FROM ETON MANOR...
TO THE OLYMPICS

First published in 2010 by Libri Publishing

Copyright © Jim Lewis

ISBN 978 1 907471 03 2

A CIP catalogue record for this book is available from The British Library

Design by Helen Taylor

Maps by Alice Gadney of Silver7 Mapping Ltd

Printed in the UK by Ashford Colour Press

Libri Publishing
Brunel House
Volunteer Way
Faringdon
Oxfordshire
SN7 7YR

Tel: +44 (0)845 873 3837
www.libripublishing.co.uk

FROM ETON MANOR
TO THE OLYMPICS

more Lea Valley secrets revealed

Jim Lewis

LIBRI
PUBLISHING

Wright's Flour Mill c. 1950

SPONSOR PROFILE

Libri Publishing was supported in the publication of this book by G.R. Wright & Sons Ltd., The Flour Millers.

The baking trade has bought flour from Ponders End Mill on the River Lea since 1086. The Wright family have milled there since 1867, specialising in making the very best quality flours and it is now London's only mill and Enfield's oldest business.

With its 17th-century mill, flanked by a Georgian mill house and Georgian offices, and close by, a 16th-century great barn and numerous other listed buildings, Ponders End Mills is one of the most complete groupings of historical industrial buildings still being worked in Greater London. This rare survivor is set within meadows bisected by a tributary of the River Lea, and is something of an oasis in Ponders End's industrial landscape. However, appearances can be deceptive, as behind the historic facade is a large, modern food factory, which operates to standards of quality and hygiene to satisfy the most discerning of clients.

When George Wright first came to Ponders End Mills some 140 years ago, he established a simple business principle – products which were to bear his name would be made with only the finest ingredients, using the most modern techniques. Four generations later, his great, great grandson David Wright is still following this principle.

www.wrightsflour.co.uk

DEDICATION

This book is dedicated to my family and also to my late mother and father, Leonora Maud Lewis and Walter Harry Portman Lewis.

ABOUT THE AUTHOR

Dr Jim Lewis has spent most of his career in the consumer electronics industry, apart from a three-year spell in the Royal Air Force servicing airborne and ground wireless communications equipment. When working in the Lea Valley for Thorn EMI Ferguson he represented the company abroad on several occasions and was involved in the exchange of manufacturing technology. Currently he is a Consultant to Terry Farrell & Partners on the historical development of London's Lea Valley and a Workers' Educational Association (WEA) tutor teaching industrial history. He also teaches students within the Community Programme who have learning difficulties. A freelance writer, researcher and broadcaster for his specialist subject – London's Lea Valley – he also has a genuine passion for encouraging partnership projects within the local community, which in the long term are planned to help stimulate social and economic regeneration. Dr Lewis is married with four grown-up children and lives in Lincolnshire.

The author Dr Jim Lewis cutting the ribbon, with the Director of the Pump House Steam & Transport Museum Trust, Lindsay Collier MA, to open a special exhibition commemorating the 90th anniversary of the birth of the Associated Equipment Company (AEC), Walthamstow, the company responsible for the founding of London Transport (now Transport for London). Lindsay Collier and the Pump House Steam & Transport Museum Trust are responsible for designing and promoting the *Lea Valley Experience* project.

SERIES ACKNOWLEDGEMENTS

The author wishes to thank the following organisations, companies and societies for their encouragement, support and advice and for supplying many of the illustrations within this book:

Alexandra Palace and Park Trust, Wood Green, London
BAE Systems, Farnborough, Hampshire
Bishopsgate Institute, London
Black & Ethnic Minority Business Association, Walthamstow, London
BOC Process Plants, Edmonton, London
Brooklands Museum, Weybridge, Surrey
Bruce Castle Museum, Tottenham, London
Civix, Exton Street, London
Corporation of Trinity House, Tower Hill, London
Cuffley Industrial Heritage Society, Cuffley, Hertfordshire
Edmonton Hundred Historical Society, Enfield, Middlesex
Enfield Archaeological Society, Enfield, Middlesex
Enfield Business Centre, Enfield, Middlesex
Enfield Energy Centre Limited, Enfield, Middlesex
Enfield Enterprise Agency, Enfield, Middlesex
Enfield Local History Unit, Enfield, Middlesex
English Heritage, Blandford Street, London
Epping Forest Museum, Waltham Abbey, Essex
Greater London Record Office, Northampton Road, London
Gunpowder Mills Study Group, Guildford, Surrey
Guy & Wright Ltd., Green Tye, Hertfordshire
Hackney Society, Hackney, London
Harper Collins Publishers, Hammersmith, London
Hawker Siddeley Power Transformers, Walthamstow, London
Historical Publications Ltd., Barnsbury, London
Hornsey Historical Society, Hornsey, London
House of Lords Record Office, Westminster, London
Imperial War Museum, Duxford, Cambridgeshire
Institution of Civil Engineers, George Street, London
Institution of Engineering and Technology, Savoy Place, London
Institution of Mechanical Engineers, Birdcage Walk, London
Jewish Museum, Finchley, London
John Higgs, Freelance Historian, Fairford, Gloucestershire
Johnson Matthey, Enfield, Middlesex
Lea Valley Growers Association, Cheshunt, Hertfordshire
Lee Valley Business and Innovation Centre, Enfield, Middlesex
Lee Valley Regional Park Authority, Enfield, Middlesex
London Borough of Enfield, Enfield, Middlesex
London Borough of Haringey, Haringey, London
London Borough of Newham, East Ham, London
London Borough of Waltham Forest, Walthamstow, London
London Lee Valley Partnership Limited, Great Eastern Street, London
London Organising Committee of the Olympic & Paralympic Games, Canary Wharf, London
London Waste Ltd, Edmonton, London
Lotus Engineering, Hethel, Norwich, Norfolk
Marconi Archive, Oxford University Library Services, Oxford, Oxfordshire

Markfield Beam Engine & Museum, Tottenham, London
Midland Publishing Limited, Earl Shilton, Leicester
Ministry of Defence Library, Royal Armouries, Leeds, Yorkshire
Museum of London, London Wall, London
National Archive, Kew, Richmond, Surrey
National Army Museum, Chelsea, London
National Maritime Museum, Greenwich, London
National Portrait Gallery, London
Natural History Museum, Kensington, London
Navtech Systems Ltd., Market Harborough, Leicestershire
New River Action Group, Hornsey, London
Newham Local History Library, Stratford, London
North London Strategic Alliance, Wood Green, London
Perkins Group, Leyton, London
Phillips Auctioneers & Valuers, New Bond Street, London
Potters Bar Historical Society, Potters Bar, Hertfordshire
Pump House Steam & Transport Museum, Walthamstow, London
RCHME Cambridge, (National Monuments Record), Cambridge, Cambridgeshire
Reuters Limited, Fleet Street, London
River Lea Tidal Mill Trust, Bromley-by-Bow, London
Royal Air Force Museum, Hendon, London
Royal Commission on Historic Manuscripts, Quality Court, Chancery Lane, London
Royal Society of Chemistry, Burlington House, London
Royal Television Society, Holborn Hall, London
Science Museum, Kensington, London
Scout Association, Chingford, Essex
Southgate District Civic Trust, Southgate, London
Speedway Museum, Broxbourne, Hertfordshire
Stratford City Challenge, Stratford, London
Tesco, Cheshunt, Hertfordshire
Thames Water, Reading, Berkshire
Thorn EMI Archive, Hayes, Middlesex
Tower Hamlets Local History Library, Tower Hamlets, London
University of Leicester Space Research Group, Leicester, Leicestershire
Upper Lee Valley Partnership, Tottenham Hale, London
Valley Grown Nurseries, Nazeing, Essex
Vauxhall Heritage, Luton, Bedfordshire
Eric Verdon-Roe, grandson of Alliott Verdon-Roe
Vestry House Museum, Walthamstow, London
Waltham Abbey Royal Gunpowder Mills Company Ltd., Waltham Abbey, Essex
Walthamstow Amateur Cine Video Club, Walthamstow, London
WEA, London District, Luke Street, London
Wordsworth Editions, Ware, Hertfordshire

While many individuals have freely given their knowledge, some unknowingly, which
has contributed greatly to the production of this series of books, I have, on a number
of occasions paid special tribute to certain people in the footnotes of various
chapters.

I could not let the occasion pass without recording my sincere thanks to my wife
Jenny for her superb editorial skills and outstanding patience. The author freely
admits that this voluntary sacrifice on Jenny's part has comprehensively tested the
cement that holds our wonderful marriage together.

AUTHOR'S NOTE

Events such as the Olympics can be brought into our homes and workplaces from the host country as they take place through the power of electronic communication – radio, television, the Internet and satellite broadcasts. The technology that allowed this to happen was first discovered and developed at Ponders End, Enfield in London's Lea Valley.

In November 1904, after much experiment, Professor Ambrose Fleming registered his patent for the diode valve, the world's first thermionic device. This inspired invention not only paved the way for today's multimedia electronics industry, but also created the delivery platform for space travel, e-mail and the Internet, not to mention computers.

Thirty-two years after Fleming's invention, in November 1936, the world's first high-definition public service television broadcasts were transmitted by the BBC from Alexandra Palace, positioned on the crest of the Lea Valley's western slopes.

Centring the 2012 Olympic and Paralympic Games in London's Lea Valley will provide a unique opportunity to remind the world that it was the development of electronic communication within the region that has allowed the participating nations to share the message of peace and friendship.

Jim Lewis

CONTENTS

INTRODUCTION

It is probably fair to say that authors who research interesting and little-known historical subjects tend to resist the requests of their readers to produce yet another book highlighting new facts. Then, as in my case, the pressure becomes too great and the research bullet has to be bitten. Once the decision is made there is no turning back and the author is faced with months, sometimes years, of archive research to follow up reader leads and to see if sufficient material exists in a particular subject area to construct an interesting and worthwhile story. While the prospect of the challenge at first may appear daunting, once fully committed and immersed in the work the excitement level builds and it is particularly satisfying when new information comes to light.

In my last three books, I invited readers, particularly teachers and school children, to get involved in Lea Valley projects and also to take on the role of detectives to discover if more interesting stories existed about the region. Some schools and universities rose to the challenge and on a number of occasions I was invited to become involved and also to act as a Lea Valley tour guide. It is occasions like these that make writing doubly rewarding.

Due to considerable local interest, and also the requests by many retailers for reprints of earlier material, the author has been persuaded to deviate from the intentions of the original format used in my earlier Lea Valley books, that of keeping chapters deliberately short, and for this new series I shall include a fuller treatment of many of the subjects. Therefore, it is intended to give each book in the series a particular theme. In this way it is hoped that that the readers' requests will be largely satisfied and also a greater insight into the developments of the region will be achieved.

I have been greatly encouraged to be quoted by prominent writers and broadcasters such as Ian Sinclair and also to receive letters from Dr Adam Hart-Davis saying "I had no idea that the great George Parker Bidder was, no less, 'the maker of modern West Ham'. I told the story in the wilds of Moretonhampstead." The BBC newscaster Mike Embly, once referred to me as the "Lea Valley alarm clock" as

I appear to wake people up to the historic significance of the region. These compliments make the long hours in front of a computer screen and the many years of archive research seem worthwhile and this encourages me to discover and write more about the Lea Valley, its entrepreneurs and its world firsts. Perhaps, sometime in the future the region will no longer be Britain's best-kept secret.

As I am mindful that the forthcoming Olympics will bring many people to the Lea Valley from around the world, who will want to learn a little more about the region, I have decided to include some stories to attract those readers with broader interests beyond that of the subject of industrial heritage.

Jim Lewis

1. FROM ETON MANOR TO THE OLYMPICS

O n 6 July 2005 in Singapore, the International Olympic Committee announced that London had won the bid to host the Olympic and Paralympic Games in the year 2012. As the result was announced television crews began interviewing weary, yet ecstatic British officials, who up until then had spent every available moment putting the finishing touches to their bid presentation. Not all, it would seem, had believed that London could pull off this nail-biting win against what many pundits claimed to be the favoured city, Paris. When the television cameras cut to the waiting crowds at Stratford, in London's East End, watchers could not fail to be moved by the scenes of sheer excitement as local residents came to realise that the Games' major facilities would be located on their doorstep in the lower Lea Valley, an area that over the years had seen more than its fair share of industrial dereliction and neglect. For decades, the region had been crying out for a regeneration stimulus of this magnitude and it would seem that the dreams of local people were about to be realised.

By a quirky coincidence, the opening of the 2012 Games in the lower Lea Valley will re-establish a 64-year-old link with the post-war Olympics, which London hosted in 1948, at the former Wembley Stadium.

To explain how this remarkable story came about we have to go

Captain Gerald Wellesley MC (1885–1972), of the Oxfordshire Yeomanry, at Ypres in 1915. Wellesley founded the Eton Old Boys' Club at Hackney Wick in 1909.

back to the year 1907, to a place called Hackney Wick, in the lower Lea Valley. It was there that the young Gerald Wellesley, a grandson of the Duke of Wellington and an Old Etonian came to live. It is difficult to appreciate why a man from such a privileged background, who had attended one of the world's most exclusive schools, Eton College, established by King Henry VI in 1440, would wish to make his home in an area of London far removed from his upper class roots.

Wellesley appears to have been a man with a purpose who had observed that working-class boys and young men from London's East End had little opportunity for further education and amusement in their spare time and he was determined to do something about it. At the time, those in employment worked a ten- to twelve-hour day with up to eight hours on a Saturday. There was normally an hour for lunch but no tea breaks. Holidays, for those in factories, amounted to a one-week shutdown per year, for which workers received no pay.

Wellesley first worked with the Eton Mission Boys' Club, which catered for boys up to their late teens. The Club had been set up by the Eton Mission, an organisation established by Old Etonians in 1880 to work in the East End of London. After a while Wellesley decided there was a need for what can best be described as an extension to the Mission's facilities that would provide young people with opportunities to take part in sporting as well as educational activities. In so doing he hoped to bring them fulfilment and brighten up their otherwise humdrum existence. We can be quite clear of Wellesley's intentions as these are laid out in an article published in 1960. Here he explains that "about 1908, I realised that it made little sense to accustom boys to Club life and 'team spirit' if, at the age of 18 or 19, they were turned away from the Club 'base' around which their lives were centred. Accordingly, during 1909, the Eton Old Boys' club was formed – independently of the Mission – and in the autumn of that year opened its doors at the corner of Daintry Street to former members of the Eton Mission Boys' Club." This might imply that Wellesley had a difference of opinion regarding the leisure and educational needs of this particular group of young men with those who were running the Mission.

Although not politically correct today, it is interesting to read the language contained in an early Club annual report, so I shall reproduce the leading paragraph verbatim.

> The Boys' Club, which is only one of the many institutions for lads in Hackney Wick, is run for the very roughest class of

working boy, and as we look back on the past twelve months, though we have at the same time every reason to be satisfied with the progress made, yet we find ourselves face to face with the danger that our Club may become so respectable as to keep away the ragged street-arab, with whom we try so hard to keep in touch. It is not so much that the appearance of the boys themselves has altered in any appreciable degree, as that an atmosphere of order and self-respect has grown up in the Club.

The Wellesley initiative of setting up the Old Boys' section seems to have been the catalyst for the Mission Council's decision to concentrate their resources on enlarging their church, rather than expanding the Club's facilities. Responsibility for the younger boys' section, that was obviously popular with the local youth, was taken over by Wellesley and run independently of the Mission. The expansion placed great strain on the limited accommodation at Daintry Street so Wellesley sought wealthy sponsors to fund his next, highly ambitious, project. He was obviously successful in his endeavours, as by July 1913 a purpose-built complex was constructed in Riseholme Street, Hackney Wick, to accommodate the ever-growing number of applicants eager to join the Club.

Typical East End boys that Gerald Wellesley wished to help, being classed by him as "raw material".

We are given a clue to Wellesley's character and great determination when he modestly describes his stoic efforts to acquire the land on which Hackney Wick Farm and Manor House stood, so that he could build his ambitious premises for the boys, as "protracted negotiations". There is no doubt that Wellesley was well connected and able to call upon his many Old Etonian friends and others in high places for help in realising his dream. This is evidenced by the fact that Field Marshal Lord Roberts, V.C., who had accepted the Presidency of the Clubs, conducted the opening ceremony at Riseholme Street.

The purchase of the old farm at Hackney Wick brought together the names of Eton and Manor, hence the origin of the Eton Manor Clubs. Eton Manor is a name very much alive today, as local people will know from the various sporting activities taking place in and around Waltham Forest under that name. From the beginning the Clubs, which operated as separate sections under the one umbrella, offered a wide range of activities,

The original Old Boys' Club in Daintry Street, Hackney Wick.

both sports and educational. The choices on offer grew year on year and catered for new interests as their popularity increased. In education several different subjects were taught including maths, English, music and first aid. The boys could also join discussion groups in dramatics and general knowledge. Professional tutors from Eton College and elsewhere were brought in to teach the different subjects and the boys also had use of a well-stocked library with a reference section. Those who wished to participate in sports and games were also well catered for, as experienced coaches were on hand to teach the most popular disciplines. These ranged from table tennis to athletics.

The year after Riseholme Street opened, Britain was plunged into the Great War and, as might be imagined, this had a considerable effect upon the Club. Many young men and managers of official

The derelict Manor Farm site at Hackney Wick in 1912, before the building of the new Riseholme Street complex.

The newly built complex of Eton Manor Clubs in Riseholme Street, Hackney Wick, as they appeared in 1913.

military age, and some who were too young to be called up for military service, enlisted in the armed forces. Over 200 from the Club saw service in the armed forces, of whom 21 sadly lost their lives.

Despite the setbacks brought about by the First, and later the Second World War, the Clubs produced many notable athletes, several achieving international status in athletics, football, rugby, boxing and swimming. For the Clubs to have lasted so long while

Some of the facilities on offer at the new Riseholme Street complex.

THE ETON

OLD BOYS BILLIARD ROOM.

THE BIG HALL.

BOYS' CLUBS HACKNEY WICK N.E.

THE BAR.

VIEW FROM MANOR HOUSE GARDEN.

maintaining their immense popularity (often youngsters had to join waiting lists) was due to the continuing hard work and enthusiasm of a dedicated band of supporters and sponsors who carried on in Wellesley's tradition. Although there were many notable benefactors, supporters and helpers, it would be highly remiss not to mention the late Les Golding, secretary of the athletic club for over half a century, and also the philanthropy of the late Major Arthur Villiers whose name lives on in the Villiers Park Educational Trust.

The early 1930s saw the Club acquire some 32 acres of rough ground on Hackney Marshes adjacent to Ruckholt Road, Leyton, on which a number of half-filled-in pits were located. Here was established a sports ground that became known as 'The Wilderness', which no doubt described the depressing look of the area at the time. Over the years 'The Wilderness' was transformed into a sports complex of some nine football pitches, two rugby pitches, six tennis courts, several cricket pitches, a squash court, a netball court and also a bowling green. The facilities at Leyton grew into some of the most extensive and prestigious in Britain, boasting a well-equipped gymnasium, a running track, a splash pool, a physiotherapy room and a stadium. Also available were changing rooms, shower and bathrooms, two canteens and a pavilion building. As a sign that the Club was moving with the times, and for those who wished to dabble in transport maintenance, a motor-scooter workshop was built to cater for the many young people who had become more affluent than those who had joined the Club in the early years.

Arthur George Childs-Villiers DSO, DL (1883–1969), one of the most philanthropic supporters of the Eton Manor Clubs. On 31 October 1951 Villiers was granted the Honorary Freedom of the Borough of Leyton.

Returning to the story of the first Olympic connection with London's Lea Valley will bring us to the time of the Second World War, when the military, who were allowed to commandeer land, placed huts on the Eton Manor athletics track. According to Les Golding this was a cinder track that had been laid in 1936, on ground adjacent to "The Wilderness". Apparently the Club had acquired the ground that had once been a football pitch belonging to a local public house, on which a semi-professional team had

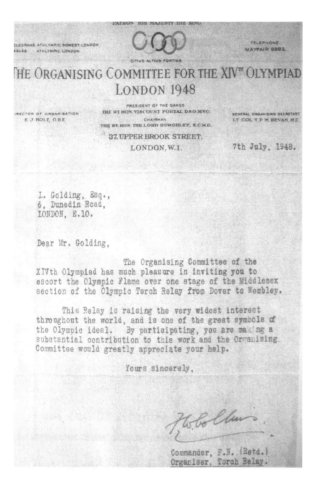

PATRON HIS MAJESTY THE KING

TELEGRAMS ATHLYMPIC SOWEST LONDON
ABLES ATHLYMPIC LONDON

TELEPHONE
MAYFAIR 8882

CITIUS ALTIUS FORTIUS

THE ORGANISING COMMITTEE FOR THE XIVth OLYMPIAD
LONDON 1948

PRESIDENT OF THE GAMES
DIRECTOR OF ORGANISATION   THE RT HON VISCOUNT PORTAL D.S.O.MVO
E. J HOLT, O.B.E   CHAIRMAN   GENERAL ORGANISING SECRETARY
                  THE RT HON. THE LORD BURGHLEY, K.C.M.G.   LT COL. T P M BEVAN M.C

97, UPPER BROOK STREET,
LONDON, W.1.   7th July, 1948.

L. Golding, Esq.,
6, Dunedin Road,
LONDON, E.10.

Dear Mr. Golding,

The Organising Committee of the
XIVth Olympiad has much pleasure in inviting you to
escort the Olympic Flame over one stage of the Middlesex
section of the Olympic Torch Relay from Dover to Wembley.

This Relay is raising the very widest interest
throughout the world, and is one of the great symbols of
the Olympic ideal. By participating, you are making a
substantial contribution to this work and the Organising
Committee would greatly appreciate your help.

Yours sincerely,

Commander, F.N. (Retd.)
Organiser, Torch Relay.

A letter from the Organising Committee for the XIV Olympiad, London 1948, inviting Les Golding of the Eton Manor Athletic Club to escort the Olympic flame over the Middlesex stage of the Dover to Wembley torch relay.

played. After the War, the returning officials and Club members discovered, to their horror, that the huts, which were still there towards the end of 1948, had caused considerable damage to the track's surface. By luck or good fortune, the redundant track surface from the 1948 Olympic Games at Wembley was uplifted and transported to Leyton and used, with the help of volunteer members, to repair the Eton Manor track. As a schoolboy, in the early 1950s, the author ran on this track, achieving one of his best mile times. At the time, the tale of the Olympic track circulated amongst local athletes and its veracity was never questioned.

When writing this story of the Olympic track I thought it prudent to find documentary evidence to support the claim that it really did come from Wembley after the 1948 Games. However, this proved to be a more difficult task than first anticipated. Hours were spent in the Waltham Forest archives viewing rolls of microfilm that contained back copies of local newspapers of the time, all to no avail. Correspondence was carried out with national athletic bodies and again no clues were forthcoming. Even Dr Roger Bannister, who had run on the track, was contacted through his agent and the message came back "I have spoken to Sir Roger and unfortunately he is not able to shed any light on this matter, as it is not something that he has heard of before".

Almost in desperation I contacted an old Eton Manor running colleague, Tom Everitt, who had also heard the tale but had not seen any documentary evidence to confirm the story. However, he kindly volunteered to go through back copies of *Chin Wag*, the magazine of the Eton Manor Clubs, to see if anything could be found. Two weeks later a letter from Tom arrived with a photocopy of a page from the January *Chin Wag* of 1949 and tucked away at the bottom of page four, was the evidence I had been seeking. Here was a short unattributed article where the author was gently berating certain

Club members for their seeming lack of enthusiasm for manual toil.
The piece went on to state:

> One would expect that with such good fortune as procuring
> the Olympic track we would be inundated with volunteers to
> lay it. All that is required is one hour's work from each Harrier,
> but to date only 30 members have come forward. We do not
> wish to raise blushes by printing the names of the absentees,
> and hope that those who have not done their bit will get down
> to it at once. Gaffers Dicky and Dodger are on duty every Sunday
> morning. Those blokes, who in the two middle weeks of August
> spent many hours in running round the track in an endeavour
> to get fit in fourteen days will also be welcome.

We may never find out how the 1948 Olympic track came to Eton
Manor, although I suspect that there could still be a few people
around who have the answer. However, one might speculate that it
was due to members like the late Club secretary, Les Golding, who
had been a member of the Olympic torch-carrying relay. This would
have probably given him access to Olympic officials and a deal
could have been brokered. Les was not the sort of man to pass up
an opportunity, especially if he could gain something for his
beloved athletic club.

There is no doubt that the coming of the Olympic track to Leyton
acted as a catalyst for greater things. In 1951 Eton Manor was the
first Club in Britain to be equipped with floodlights and also the

Les Golding, second from the
left in the banded Eton
Manor vest, escorting the
Olympic torch to Wembley in
1948.

first to host a floodlit athletics meeting. The Club was also the first to have raised landing areas for the high jump and pole vault and also the first to be equipped with an all-weather take-off for the jumpers. Having such modern facilities attracted many of the countries leading post-war athletes to the track. Notable amongst them was a young medical student, Roger Bannister who, in July 1954, became the first athlete in the world to break the four-minute mile barrier, the Holy Grail of athletics. Another famous name, who was later to found the London Marathon and become a prominent athlete in his own right, and who assisted Bannister on his record-breaking run, was the late Chris Brasher. In 1956 Brasher claimed gold for Britain when he won the 3,000 metres steeplechase at the Melbourne Olympics.

Chris Brasher (No. 27) clearing the water-jump at a floodlit meeting held on the former 1948 Olympic track at Eton Manor sports ground, Ruckholt Road, Leyton (early 1950s). In 1956, Brasher won a gold medal for Britain in the 3,000 metres steeplechase at the Melbourne Olympics.

E.M. Bailey (No. 3) winning the 100 yards from B. Shelton (No. 10) and A. Pilkington (No. 5) at a floodlit meeting at the Eton Manor sports ground, 1951.

E.M. Bailey, one of the fastest
post-war sprinters in Britain,
pictured at a floodlit meeting
at the Eton Manor sports
ground c.1951.

Joy Jordan (No. 51) winning
the women's 880 yards at a
floodlit meeting at the Eton
Manor sports ground in 1951;
Madeline Ibbotson (No. 53),
Phyllis Purkins (No. 56) and
June Byatt (No. 57).

The year 1967 was a sad time for the Eton Manor Clubs. A compulsory purchase order was placed on Riseholme Street and the buildings were eventually demolished to make way for the A102(M) East Cross Route that links the East End of London to Kent via the Blackwall tunnel. A slight clue still remains to the whereabouts of the former Hackney Wick headquarters in the name of Riseholme Gate, an entrance to Victoria Park in Cadogan Terrace, which is sited opposite where the Club once stood.

Due to increasing pressure from other development schemes, the Eton Manor Clubs could no longer use the Wilderness Sports Ground in Leyton and the Trustees eventually decided to disband the Clubs. However, a group of enthusiastic members came together who were determined to ensure that Gerald Wellesley's legacy should not fade into oblivion. The Eton Manor Association was created and it was agreed that each of the former Eton Manor Clubs should, in the future, be run independently. In the words of

The stand and spectators at the Eton Manor sports ground, early 1950s.

George Merton, the then secretary of the Eton Manor Old Boys' Association, "the time has come for the sections to look after themselves". While the loss of the prodigious Wilderness sporting facilities was a considerable setback to the athletes of the region, many of the clubs did manage to continue independently and have done so to this day, offering local people a range of healthy activities. On 30 January 1975 the Lee Valley Regional Park Authority, which had been established after the Lee Valley Regional Park Bill had received Royal Assent in December 1966, assumed responsibility for the old Wilderness Sports Ground, more popularly known in recent times as Eton Park.

The Eton Manor sports ground from the air, 1962. To the middle right of the picture can be seen the 1948 Olympic track that was re-laid after the Games at Wembley. In the foreground is Ruckholt Road, Leyton.

The announcement of the Olympic and Paralympic Games coming to the Lea Valley is already encouraging young people within the region to participate in sporting activities in the hope of representing their country in 2012. Interestingly, the future arrival of the Olympics bears an uncanny resemblance to Gerald Wellesley's vision for London's East End – that of providing first-class sporting and educational facilities for the region's young people. So in a way, the building of the Olympic stadium, with its complementary amenities, will deliver a range of new facilities to the lower Lea Valley that will replace those that were destroyed in the late 1960s to make way for other schemes. When the Games are over, the authorities have agreed that much of the infrastructure that is left will be developed in an imaginative way for others to enjoy. The Olympic 2012 legacy can be viewed as a fitting epitaph for those early pioneers such as Gerald Wellesley by continuing their visionary initiative of providing the best athletic facilities for London's East End, that will enthuse, encourage and give support to our young people for decades to come.

An aerial view of the Olympic stadium, taken November 2008.

A picture of the 2012 Olympic Stadium, one-third completed, taken from the platform of the DLR Station, Pudding Mill Lane, April 2009.

An indicative map of the Olympic Park.

An artist's impression of the Olympic Stadium.

REFERENCES

Author unknown, *A Brief Description of the Background to the Lee Valley Park and the Park Authority*, Lee Valley Regional Park Authority, October, 2005.

Author unknown, "Harriers' Notes", *Chin Wag*, The Magazine of the Eton Manor Clubs, January, 1949.

Author unknown, *Eton Manor Association Youth Club*, Newsletter.

Author unknown, *The Story of Eton Manor in Hackney Wick and Leyton*, c.1962.

Conversation with Ms Liz Loly of the Lee Valley Regional Park Authority, 4 December, 2005.

Dunn, Michael, General Article, *Eton Manor Association*, No. 7, February, 1971.

Email in possession of author from the Archivist of Eton College, 29 September, 2005.

Golding, Les, "Eton Manor Athletic Club 50 Years", *International Sports Fellowship Bulletin*, 1972.

Interview with ex-Siemens worker, the late Leonora Lewis, Attlee Terrace, Walthamstow, London, (10/7/88).

Letter in possession of author from PBJ Management, 18 October, 2005.

Wellesley, Gerald, *The Story of the Early Days of the Eton Manor Clubs*, 1960.

Note

The author would like to thank Tom Everitt and the members of Eton Manor Athletic Club for providing documentary material for this chapter. Also I am grateful to the London Organising Committee of the Olympic Games (LOCOG) for granting permission to reproduce the images of the proposed Olympic facilities for the 2012 Games. I should also like to thank the Lee Valley Regional Park Authority, the Vestry House Museum, Eton College, Bishopsgate Institute and the Villiers Park Educational Trust for their guidance and helpful suggestions.

2. TIME TRAVEL THROUGH LONDON'S LEA VALLEY AND PARK – FROM PREHISTORY TO THE NORMANS

Often, when giving talks on the industries of the Lea Valley, I am asked to explain how the region came to be formed. Questions are also raised about those early people who came to the region to conquer and settle. To do these requests justice would require a very weighty tome indeed, but in the following few hundred words I shall try to describe how the valley came to be.

It has been estimated that the earth is 4,600,000,000 years old. Compared to this, the Lea Valley, which was formed 1,000,000 to 1,800,000 years ago, during the four glaciations (ice ages) of the Pleistocene Epoch, is a mere newcomer. The last ice sheet (which geologists have calculated advanced from the north to a line that extended west-east across Britain from south Wales through Finchley to south Essex) retreated 10,000 years ago. Water created as the ice melted (melt waters) brought down deposits of sand, gravel and clay that eventually formed the flat marshy flood plain of the lower Lea Valley. Evidence of this can be seen today in places like Walthamstow and Tottenham marshes. Indeed, we are fortunate

The ancient Walthamstow Marsh (2001), now protected as a Nature Reserve within the Lee Valley Regional Park.

that our recent ancestors named one of these areas Walthamstow Common Marsh and used it for growing hay and grazing cattle. This has allowed much of the Marsh's ancient character to remain. Since 1985 the area has been designated a Site of Special Scientific Interest (SSSI) and supports some 400 different species of insect, plant and animal.

Towards the northern end of the Lea Valley which, unlike its southern counterpart, has not remained undisturbed, there is evidence of a much earlier period going back many millions of years. During the extensive gravel excavations that took place in the 20th century, several types of fossil and a variety of prehistoric animal remains were unearthed, providing clues about the valley's early history for the archaeologists to study. The method used for extracting gravel is very much an industrial operation, which has meant that many of the ancient finds that have come to light failed to receive the same level of sensitive recording as would have been expected from a planned archaeological dig. However, on the plus side, since gravel extraction has now virtually ceased in the upper Lea Valley the aftermath has created a number of water features, which are home to a variety of animals, insects and plants – not to mention the different species of fish, which inhabit these man-made lakes now that nature has re-established herself.

A collection of animal remains, fossils and other artefacts removed from the Lea Valley and surrounding area during gravel extraction. Permission to photograph the collection was given by the directors of RMC Aggregates (Greater London) Limited.

Mammoth Tooth
On loan from St. Albans Sand and Gravel

The picture shows one of the last areas of the Lea Valley to have gravel extracted. Now, a designated nature reserve, this site near Great Amwell in Hertfordshire is attracting a wide variety of birds, plants and other wildlife.

Imagine, if you will, the Lea Valley landscape some 10,000 years ago as the ice retreated northward. It would be possible to recognise the general layout of the high ground as being similar to that of today. However, the valley slopes and floor would have looked quite different. This earlier hostile landscape, devoid of trees and having a climate akin to that of Iceland is a far cry from the present familiar topography of the Lee Valley Regional Park with its nature reserves, water features and other visitor attractions. Geological evidence suggests that the River Lea, at this time, was considerably wider than it is today, probably reaching a mile or more in places.

As the region gradually became warmer and trees and vegetation began to flourish, we come upon evidence of habitation by man. Archaeologists excavating in the 1920s just east of Broxbourne, discovered a Mesolithic (middle stone age) site (circa 6,000 BC – 3,000 BC). These early people, who appear to have been hunter-gatherers, probably came to Britain over the land bridge that linked England and France until 6,000 years ago. Indications of their existence (flint tools, animal remains and dwelling materials) were discovered buried beneath the Lea Valley peat. Further finds came to light in the 1970s when excavations at Broxbourne and Dobbs Weir revealed flint axes and a fish spear complete with flint barbs.

By around 3,000 BC the climate had warmed considerably and the Lea Valley landscape had changed from its former barren state to a more welcoming environment. Now the slopes were heavily wooded and the valley floor was covered by marshes on a bed of peat. The Neolithic (new stone age) people, who had earlier crossed the Channel to Britain, were beginning to enter the Lea Valley. These people had developed new skills that differed considerably from their Mesolithic forebears. They cleared the land, kept cattle, made pottery and planted cereals (wheat and barley). Essentially they were farmers, rather than hunter-gatherers.

A Neolithic mace displayed in Epping Forest District Museum, Sun Street, Waltham Abbey. This tool would have taken our ancestors several hundred hours to make.

The period 1,800–600 BC has been termed the Bronze Age. Here, for the first time, we see a giant leap in technology with the development of copper and bronze tools, drinking beakers and other implements. It is thought that this technology came to Britain through continental traders or possibly invaders. Finds by archaeologists, particularly in north Hertfordshire and more recently at Turnford (before the erection of the new housing estates), show that Bronze Age people were once in the region.

The beginning of the Iron Age came at around 600 BC and saw the first implements made from this new material. Iron tools were tougher and cheaper than copper or bronze. Now iron axes and ploughs tipped with iron allowed land clearance and cultivation to progress much faster than before. In the late 1960s, one of the earliest Iron Age settlements to be found in southeast England was discovered north of Ware.

A late Bronze Age gold bracelet found near Harlow in Essex by a local resident in 1993. In the various showcases of the museum can be seen Neolithic axe heads, arrow heads and also Microliths (small flakes of worked flint) that have been recovered from the area of Epping Forest.

When the Romans occupied Britain in 43 AD the Lea Valley, and what is now the Lee Valley Regional Park, would have presented the invading army with a formidable obstacle to negotiate. To reach Camulodunum (Colchester), which we know was to become an extremely important Roman garrison town, the River Lea and its marshy extremities had to be crossed. Imagine the problems that this natural barrier posed for the Roman army, complete with equipment and stores as it marched north-eastward from the area that grew to become Londinium (London) in circa 50 AD. The Roman occupation of Britain appears to have lasted until around 450 AD and it is known, from the archaeological evidence (pottery, glass,

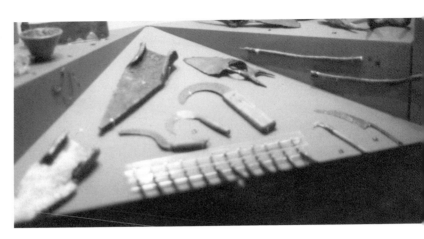

Iron tools, including plough blades and sickles on display in the Museum of London.

coins, jewellery, tools, building materials, etc.) found within the Lea Valley and the surrounding countryside that the region must have held a position of considerable strategic importance. Ermine Street led north, from the Roman settlement of Londinium directly along the valley floor to Ware, while Watling Street ran northwest to Verulamium (St Albans).

Scholars agree that the Roman occupation of Britain did not end abruptly, but gradually tailed off, allowing an overlap with the Saxon period that had begun around 400 AD. From genetic studies carried out by today's scientists, we are able to deduce that during these relatively long periods of overlap, integration of the various peoples took place. This mixing of these different cultures would have also meant the sharing of knowledge, which has probably helped mould

The remains of a Roman theatre at Verulamium, St Albans, Hertfordshire, a powerful reminder of the occupation of Britain by an advanced people.

the British character into something that outsiders see as unique.

Archaeologists have yet to find, within the boundaries of the Lee Valley Regional Park, sufficient Saxon remains to construct a complete picture of the lifestyle of these early Germanic people in the area. However, in 1972 a late Saxon hoard of some 17 artefacts was discovered in the gravels of Nazeing Marsh and in October 1987 a late Saxon log boat was unearthed from a site near the River Lea at Clapton, adjacent to Springfield Marina. Therefore, it is hoped that the future will yield more finds that will further add to our knowledge.

By turning to the Anglo-Saxon Chronicle, written between the ninth and tenth centuries AD we discover references to the next invaders, the Vikings (or Danes), who, by the ninth century, were active in the Lea Valley. In 886 AD, a bitter battle had taken place between the Saxons and Danes, which resulted in Alfred recapturing London. Afterwards, Alfred made an agreement with the Danish King Guthrum and a boundary was established between their respective territories. To achieve this, an imaginary line was draw along the Thames from the North Sea and then up the River Lea to its source. According to the Chronicle, in the year 894 AD a large Viking fleet sailed up the River Thames and then up the River Lea to a point 20 miles north of London where a fortified camp was built with ditches and ramparts. It is recorded that King Alfred (of Wessex) deprived the Danes of escape by blocking, and possibly lowering, the river. The Danes abandoned their camp, leaving their boats behind, and escaped by sending their women and children across country to East Anglia while the men marched overland to Bridgnorth in Shropshire.

A late Saxon hoard of iron and copper-alloy artefacts, including a three-pronged fish spear, discovered at Nazeing, Essex in the early 1970s.

Today's casual visitor to the Lee Valley Regional Park would probably find it difficult to imagine the events that took place in this relatively small area of land adjacent to the capital that helped shape a future British nation. It might also be hard to imagine, while taking a leisurely stroll in the now much-altered and landscaped Park, that the east bank of the River Lea was once Danish territory (Danelaw) while the west bank was Saxon (Wessex).

A skull of a Saxon woman, who is thought to have been over 45 years old, discovered in an ancient cemetery in Sun Street, Waltham Abbey.

The influence of the Norman Conquest in 1066 on the Lea Valley region has left much material evidence for our visitor to see. Apart from the recording of several Lea Valley mills in the Domesday survey of 1086, there is also much remaining architecture be observed. For example, the church at Waltham Abbey (the Abbey Church of Waltham Holy Cross and St. Lawrence), although much altered over the centuries, has several fine Norman features. These include arches, a north and south door and a nave. Harold, Earl of Wessex, who later became the last Saxon King of England, founded the church circa 1060. After Harold's death, at the battle of Hastings in 1066, it is said that his body was brought to Waltham Abbey for burial. There is currently a stone slab that stands to the east of the church that marks the grave. However, historians and archaeologists have suggested that the placing of the stone may be inaccurate, as Harold's body was reputedly moved on at least three different occasions.

The restored Oseberg Viking ship, estimated to have been built around 800 AD. Had the Vikings come up the River Lea, as suggested in the Anglo-Saxon Chronicle, they would have probably used ships of a similar type.

A statue of King Alfred, carved in the mid-19th century.

A section of the Bayeux Tapestry depicting a soldier, positioned below the name Harold, who seems to be pulling an arrow from his eye. This has caused several writers to suggest that the scene shows Harold meeting his death. Charles Gibbs-Smith, who was Keeper Emeritus at the Victoria and Albert Museum, London and an authority on the Bayeux Tapestry, has produced convincing evidence to show that the figure of the soldier could not have been Harold. Furthermore he states, when discussing the arrow-in-the-eye story, that there is no historical evidence for it at all.

The eastern end of Waltham Abbey where, it is alleged, the body of King Harold is buried. Note the semi-circular gravel path marking the original line of the Norman church

A stone marking the possible site of King Harold's grave.

REFERENCES

Ashby, Margaret, *The Book of the River Lea*, Barracuda Books Ltd., 1991.

Author unknown, *Walthamstow Marsh – a Guide to the History of the Area*, Lee Valley Regional Park Authority, 1986.

Bascombe, K.N. & Bentley, John, *A Walk Round Waltham Abbey*, Waltham Abbey Historical Society, 1998.

Batley, J., "The Compilation of the Anglo-Saxon Chronicle Once More", *Leeds Studies in English* 16, 1985.

Burnby, J.G.L. & Parker, M., *The Navigation of the River Lee (1190–1790)*, Edmonton Hundred Historical Society, Occasional Paper New Series No.36.

Camp, John & Dean, Dinah, *King Harold's Town*, Waltham Abbey Historical Society, 1988.

Gibbs-Smith, Charles H., *The Bayeux Tapestry*, Phaidon, 1973.

Heath, Cyril, *The Book of Amwell*, Barracuda Books Ltd., 1980.

Higgins, Eric, & Bascombe, Kenneth, *Waltham Abbey*, Pitkin Pictorial Ltd., 1995.

Higham, N.J., *The Norman Conquest*, Sutton Publishing Ltd., 1998.

Humble, Richard, *The Saxon Kings*, Weidenfeld and Nicolson, 1980.

Kiln, Robert, *The Dawn of History in East Herts*, The Hertfordshire Archaeological Trust, 1986.

Morris, Carole A., "A Late Saxon Hoard of Iron and Copper-Alloy Artefacts from Nazeing, Essex", *Medieval Archaeology*, Vol. XXVII, 1983.

Saklatvala, Beram, *The Origins of the English People*, David & Charles, 1969.

Savage, Anne, (trans.), *Anglo-Saxon Chronicle*, Macmillan, 1982.

Thackray, John, *The Age of the Earth*, Her Majesty's Stationery Office, 1980.

Note

The author wishes to express his sincere thanks to the Lee Valley Regional Park Authority for giving permission to reproduce a large section of the above text which was originally written (by the author) for a millennium website project.

3. FROM BIKES TO TELEVISIONS TO TIPPERS – A LEA VALLEY STORY OF SURVIVAL

It is probably not generally realised that many of the people who started businesses that are now household names began life in the embryonic 19th-century bicycle industry. William Morris (not to be confused with the similarly named William Morris – artist, writer, fabric designer, furniture designer and socialist – born in Walthamstow in 1834) but the founder of the Morris Motor Company in 1910, who went on to open his first factory in Cowley, Oxfordshire in 1913, was originally a bicycle manufacturer. In 1895 in Malda Boleslav, in today's Czech Republic, Vaclav Kelment joined with Vaclav Laurin to open a bicycle repair shop. Later their company became the now famous motorcar manufacturer, Skoda. The Wright brothers, Orville and Wilbur, the first to be credited with controlled powered flight in 1903, had opened a bicycle repair and sales shop in 1892. Later, in 1896 they formed the Wright Cycle Company to manufacture their own design of bicycles. The common thread that binds these men together is that they appear to be self-taught engineers who early on recognised the potential of both a growing bicycle market and also the development of other forms of transport that would cut down journey times.

James Perkins (1861–1927), the founder of Crownfield bicycles and J. Perkins & Son.

In 1886, before the famous names above, James Perkins (1861-1927), began a bicycle manufacturing business from the front room of his home in Crownfield Road, Leyton – now part of the London Borough of Waltham Forest. James may have acquired some of his engineering skills from his father who worked as a blacksmith. With such an engineering influence and being a keen competitive cyclist of some repute, Perkins was particularly interested in improving the design of racing bicycles, which at the time had some way to go in their development. The result was the birth of the hand-built Crownfield bicycle. The early versions had solid tyres. It should be

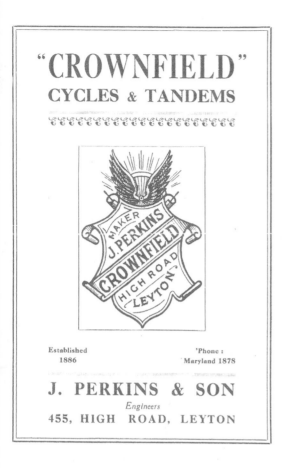

remembered that it was not until October 1888 that John Boyd Dunlop's patent gave the world "an improvement in tyres of wheels for bicycles, tricycles, or other road cars". The following year, after a tie-up with a Scottish manufacturer, the Dunlop pneumatic tyre began to be used by makers of racing bicycles.

By 1899 Perkins' bicycle building business had expanded considerably as his bikes, with their special lightweight frames, had become popular within the racing fraternity, and he started receiving orders nationally and also from around the world. To cope with the increase in demand, Perkins moved from his front room in Crownfield Road to new premises at 299 High Road, Leyton. Money was tight with many working-class people who relied on the bicycle for getting to work. Again Perkins rose to the challenge and introduced his own hire purchase agreements so that customers could pay for their bicycle over the period of one year. The earliest Perkins' agreement found by the author was dated May 1901 and the customer had signed the contract over a sixpenny Queen Victoria stamp.

Above left: The front cover of a Perkins catalogue for Crownfield cycle products, 1927.

Above right: James Perkins' first shop at 299 High Road Leyton.

"CROWNFIELD"
TANDEM. Racing and Touring

"ALL-ON" MODEL.

FRAME.	Built with Reynolds "A" Quality Tubing throughout, Tapered Round Chain and Seat Stays, each Lug Finely Tapered down to Tube, Forward Release or Hollow Spindle Type Fork Ends, Pump Hooks Brazed to Rear Centre Tube, Extra Head Oiler Fitted to side of Lug for Lubrication of Bottom Race.
WHEELS.	Single or Double Cog, Special *Guaranteed* Butted Tandem Spokes, 26 x 1½ or 1¼ Black Wheels recommended, Fitted with Ball-Bearing Wingnuts
TYRES.	Dunlop Re-inforced, Ivorycord, or to order.
SADDLES.	Brooks B17/10/19/70, etc.
MUDGUARDS.	Bluemel's "Noweights." Stay Fitting with Separate or one piece Extension.
CHAINS.	Coventry Elite or Renold Rollers.
BRAKE.	Constrictor "A" Quality.
PUMP.	Bluemel 15" x ⅞"
HANDLEBARS.	Any Patterns to order on adjustable Clips.
FINISH.	As Single Frames. (See opposite).

Chater-Lea Fittings	£18 10 0	All-on
Brampton Fittings	£17 0 0	All-on

Or Alternative Brampton, with Mansfield Racing Saddles, Renold Improved Chains, Bowden "A" Caliper, Dunlop Re-inforced Tyres, Bluemel's "Noweight" Guards and Pump.	£15 0 0 All-on

"CROWNFIELD"
FRAMES. Racing and Touring

Built with Reynolds "A" Quality Tubing throughout, Butted Steering Stem, Double Butted Fork Blades, (specially made by Reynolds) Double Butted Frame Tubes, Tapered Chain and Seat-Stays, Forward Opening or Hollow Spindle Type Rear Ends, Front Ends Solid and Machined, Slotted for Easy Release, Each Lug Finely Tapered Down to Tube, Front of Head Lugs and Crown Cut Away.

Pump Hooks Brazed on to take Bluemel Standard 15 in. Pump, Mudguard Eyes Brazed on and Chain Rest Fitted, Extra Spring Cap Oiler Fitted to Rear of Head Tube for Lubrication of Bottom Race.

Supplied Fitted with Chain Wheel and Cranks, Bracket Interiors, Head Complete, Lamp Bracket and Seat Pin. (Williams Chain Wheel and Cranks Fitted to Brampton Models).

FINISH.	Special and Highly Efficient Rust-proof Treatment. Supplied in Black and following Colours (no extra charge). Royal Blue, Harley, Olive Green, Bronze, French Grey, Cambridge Blue, Copper Bronze and Purple. Plated Fork Ends if desired.

PRICE. (LADIES OR GENTS.)

B.S.A. Fittings	-	£4 15 0
Brampton Fittings	-	£3 10 0
Chater-Lea Fittings		£4 12 6

TAPER TUBE MODELS 15/- EXTRA.

Advertisements giving the specification for Crownfield frames and tandem cycles from a Perkins catalogue first published in 1927.

Like all true entrepreneurs, Perkins did not rest on his laurels and was always on the lookout for new business opportunities. By the start of the 20th century, with the emergence of the motorcar, Perkins could see that people would want to travel longer distances faster, so he began the manufacture of motorcycles. At the time these machines were belt driven and Perkins came up with an adjustable pulley belt design that could accommodate all known motorcycle engines in Britain and Europe. The product sold across the world until overtaken by the technology of the chain drive. Not to be put off by the conventions of the day, Perkins designed a motorcycle for ladies, which was ridden by his daughter Jessie, much to the disgust of the locals, who no doubt thought that a woman's place was in the home and not gallivanting around Leyton on a noisy, new-fangled machine. James' son, Jimmy Perkins junior, was also taken up with the motorcycle craze and became a racer. He earned notoriety when in 1906, on a motorcycle built by his father, he won a five-mile handicap race, from scratch, on the relatively new Canning Town track in a fraction over six minutes three seconds. This would have equated to a quite remarkable average speed for the day of almost 50 miles per hour.

Interestingly the track at Canning Town, said to have been the best-banked motorcycle and cycle track in Britain, was established by Arnold Hills, chairman of the Thames Ironworks, with £20,000 of his own money. Hills had acquired a piece of land adjacent to the present district line between Plaistow and West Ham stations, on which was constructed a stadium, cycle track, running track, tennis courts, the largest outdoor swimming pool in England and a football pitch for his Thames Ironworks team. The Memorial Grounds, as they were known, opened on Jubilee Day 1897 to mark the 60th anniversary of Queen Victoria's reign. When the Thames Ironworks team moved to their present ground at Upton Park in 1904, they adopted the now more familiar name of West Ham United.

An unknown person posing with a belt-driven Crownfield motorcycle, c.1906.

An early postcard advertising Crownfield products.

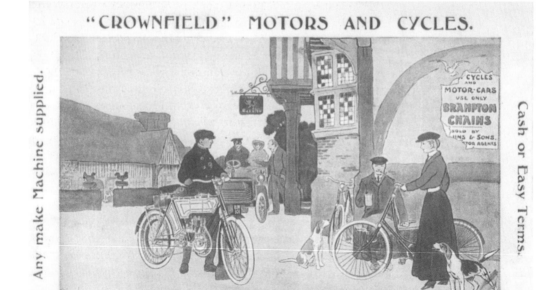

The larger shop, at 455 High Road, Leyton, which Perkins moved to in 1912 as the business expanded.

A little before the start of the First World War, in 1912, with the business still expanding, James Perkins moved to larger premises at 455 High Road, Leyton. When the conflict began in 1914, Perkins, like many other engineering businesses became involved in the manufacture of munitions. Although James Perkins was an idealist with strong pacifist beliefs, his dilemma was how to support his country in time of crisis and still maintain a clear conscience. He kept his beliefs intact by refusing payment for his war work.

On 25 January 1917, after remaining a widower for many years, James Perkins, now aged 56, married Ellen Ellis, a widow some 18 years his junior. Ellen's son Sydney was accepted into the family and took his stepfather's surname. On leaving school in 1921 young Sydney was brought into the business and within three years, in what might be concluded as the natural influence of his stepfather, took responsibility for taking the expanding business forward. In 1927 James Perkins died after building a successful business that was still flourishing after 40 years, a business that had its roots deeply embedded in club cycling. James had won the Essex Wheelers Championship on three occasions and later became President of the famous Shaftesbury Cycling Club, founded in 1888, a position he held for almost 20 years. His intimate knowledge of cycle racing allowed him to design and build bicycles, which attracted many serious club athletes to his business. So tied was Perkins to cycling that one of his employees, Dave Marsh, became the first British Road Racing Champion. Sadly, only two years after

his death, the decision was taken to phase out the custom-built Crownfield business and to concentrate on selling other manufacturers' cycles as it was soon realised that nobody could build a bicycle like James Perkins.

Under Sydney Perkins the business was still growing, much of this due to the legacy of James, who had instilled in his employees the necessity of fairness and honesty when dealing with customers, an ethos that is still present in the Perkins Group today. While carrying on the cycle and motorcycle business the company now took on motor repairs and also branched out into building vehicle bodies. As might be expected they had soon outgrown their 445 High Road address but were fortunate in acquiring adjacent land, and later the entire premises, from the Leyton Timber Company. Here a purpose-built garage was constructed.

In November 1922 the British Broadcasting Company began Britain's first wireless (radio) transmissions from Marconi House in London's Strand. Afterwards the popular craze to build your own wireless emerged and by the end of the decade was gaining momentum. Sydney Perkins spotted a business opportunity and to

Two cyclists on an early Crownfield tandem, designed and manufactured by James Perkins. The man at the front is thought to be the famous Shaftesbury Cycling Club rider, Albert Latilla.

The new pre-war purpose-built showroom and garage to accommodate cycles, radios and motor vehicles; built by the well-known Leyton builder, J. & J. Dean, on land formerly occupied by the Leyton Timber Company. Note the overhead tram wires and also the tracks on the roadway. In 1954 the showroom became a display area for new Ford and Roots Group motorcars.

accommodate the growing trend his latest venture became the erection of a new state-of-the-art showroom to display a range of radio kits, components and complete radio receivers. By the mid-1930s television broadcasts had begun from the BBC transmitter at Alexandra Palace, Wood Green and, as might be expected, Sydney embraced the new technology by adding television sales and servicing to the radio business.

When the Second World War began in September 1939 the company once again became engaged in war work. This time the vehicle side of the business took on the momentous task of maintaining almost all of the Essex Civil Defence Authority's transport in Group Seven, which accounted for over 400 vehicles. Group Seven covered the Boroughs of Barking, Chingford, Chigwell, Dagenham, Ilford, Leyton, Walthamstow, Waltham Cross, Wanstead and Woodford. Those readers with knowledge of the area will immediately appreciate the scale of the task. Although the Perkins premises – like many others in London's East End – experienced bomb damage, on the five occasions that they were hit loyal staff pulled together and the business was soon back in operation.

The post-war period saw Sydney losing no time in strengthening the business. In 1946 he oversaw the building of a large extension to the motor workshop, the construction of a new spares department and renewal of some of the ageing plant and equipment.

By the early 1950s the television business had begun to expand and, to accommodate the extra trade expected with the forthcoming coronation of Queen Elizabeth in 1953, a new showroom was opened with an innovative TV demonstration theatre in the basement. Following in the footsteps of James Perkins it was the philosophy of Sydney to ensure that talented and hardworking staff would be rewarded with promotion within the company. Maurice Dryden had joined the company in 1936 straight from school and had shown considerable enthusiasm for the radio and television business. When the new showroom opened Maurice was made director of the television business and was also given responsibility for the Perkins finance company, "Crownfield Finance".

In 1952 Harry Terry rejoined the motor vehicle side of the business as manager. Harry had previously served his apprenticeship with the engineering department of the Co-Operative Society at Stratford, east London and in 1936 he went to work for Perkins where he stayed until the outbreak of the Second World War. It was probably Sydney Perkins who had heard that Harry, a progressive and visionary man, was unsettled at his job with a major vehicle company in Romford and offered him the job at Perkins with a place on the board. This was certainly a shrewd move on Sydney's part as Harry soon began to show his worth. He quickly realised that to keep ahead of the competition, the vehicle side of the

A Perkins Rolls-Royce breakdown truck towing a Singer motorcar, c.1955. During the Leyton Carnival, Perkins regularly featured the breakdown truck in the procession.

business needed to expand rapidly. In 1954 Harry obtained a Ford car and truck franchise and another followed from the Rootes Group. Showrooms to display the new range of cars were opened in Leyton High Road, a body panel and paint shop was opened in Oliver Road, Leyton and a commercial vehicle repair workshop established at Midland Road, Leyton.

In 1960, with the vehicle business still continuing to flourish, Sydney Perkins decided to step back and take a less active role. Sydney had no family heirs so he sold his majority shares in Perkins Garages Limited to Harry Terry, although he maintained a minority holding until 1970. By the mid-1960s the post-war car market was reaching a state of over supply and dealers began cutting profit margins in the face of stiff competition. Once again the Perkins spirit of entrepreneurship shone through as Harry Terry expanded the commercial vehicle business by taking on the Anthony Hoist agency to supply and fit tipping bodies to trucks. The expansion of the business was beginning to cause space problems, which were exacerbated by the local authority placing a compulsory purchase order on the Oliver Road paint shop so that an entrance could be provided to a newly erected block of flats. However, the local authority did offer an alternative site in Rigg Approach, Leyton, adjacent to the former Lea Bridge Speedway stadium and track. Here the Perkins vehicle business consolidated their commercial operations by selling off the Leyton High Road and Midland Road sites and dividing the newly formed group, complete with administration and reception, into four sections, under one roof. These were car sales, car servicing and repair, car and light van paint and panel work and commercial vehicle repairs, servicing and bodybuilding.

In 1955 Eddie Scott, a sales representative from Hoover, joined Perkins as a sales assistant at a time when many brands of radio, television and electrical appliances were still on allocation. By the mid-1960s, with the coming of limited colour television broadcasts by the BBC the future looked decidedly bright for the go-ahead Perkins Company. It had always been the ambition of Sydney Perkins to expand the electrical side of the business but, by 1967, his health was failing and his dream was not to be realised. Now, instead of the expected expansion, the electrical business was forced to consolidate as the service department and the South Woodford shop were sold. Maurice Dryden, the director of the electrical business, left the company and Eddie Scott negotiated a management buy-out in October 1967. Although the electrical side of the business now traded under the Perkins name it was an entirely separate company. In 1969, with falling sales, mainly

The Perkins radio and television showroom and service department that opened at 617 High Road, Leyton in 1958.

induced by the increasing popularity of the motorcar, the bicycle business was forced to close. Over the next few years Sydney Perkins' health had not improved and he died in 1975, bringing to an end the Perkins family connection, but not the ethos of the founder James. Now it was the turn of Harry Terry to carry forward James' long legacy of service and customer satisfaction.

While the bicycle and television side of the business had retracted there was certainly no evidence of the trend in the commercial vehicle section. As sometimes happens in commerce, the inspiration for a new business opportunity can emerge from an everyday casual conversation. On one such day in 1968 a conversation took place between Harry Terry, his son Ian (now Chairman and Managing Director of the Perkins Group) and his general manager, Jim Jacobs. Harry had come up with the idea of carrying out modifications to the popular Ford Transit truck to convert it into a tipper. Once the idea had been fully discussed, the Perkins vehicle section set about developing the project with enthusiasm. The immediate problem to overcome was the Transit's lack of supplementary power to drive a hydraulic pump for lifting the load-carrying body section. This was achieved by combining electric motors from CAV (now Lucas CAV, a subsidiary of Lucas Aerospace Limited) with hydraulic pumps manufactured by Gowing Engineering Limited, a Company originally set up by Harry Terry.

Eddie Scott in the Perkins 617 High Road, Leyton showroom. In October 1967, Mr Scott negotiated a management buy-out of the Perkins radio, television and electrical retail business.

A page from a Perkins 1950s radio and television catalogue. Note the wording below the Ferguson television 941T claiming "excellent photographic quality".

FERGUSON 208U

4 VALVE SUPERHET, 3 WAVEBAND, SELF-CONTAINED AERIAL. IVORY CABINET. 3 WATTS UNDISTORTED OUTPUT, FOR A.C. OR D.C.

12 Guineas or on H.P. Terms

30/0 deposit & 3/4 weekly or 14/5 monthly.
£3 ,, 2/10 ,, ,, 12/3 ,,
£5 ,, 2/3 ,, ,, 9/9 ,,

FERGUSON 269 RG

CONSOLE RADIOGRAM

IN ATTRACTIVE WALNUT CABINET WITH 3 WAVEBAND CHASSIS AND 8 in. SPEAKER. CHANGER TAKES EIGHT 10 in. OR 12 in. RECORDS *MIXED* IN DRAWER.

47 Guineas or on H.P.

£3 deposit & 14/1 weekly or 61/0. monthly.
£6 ,, 13/2 ,, ,, 57/0 ,,
£10 ,, 12/0 ,, . 52/0 ,,

PERKINS say :
"FINE SETS THESE FERGUSON'S"

FERGUSON 217 RG

THIS INSTRUMENT INCORPORATES IN A BEAUTIFULLY FIGURED WALNUT CABINET, A GOOD 5 VALVE, 3 WAVE-BAND RADIO WITH AN AUTOMATIC RECORD CHANGER FOR EIGHT 10 in. OR 12 in. RECORDS.

68 Guineas or on H.P. Terms.

£8 deposit & 19/3 weekly or 83/5 monthly
£12 ,, 18/1 ,, ,, 78/4 ,,
£16 ,, 16/10 ,, ,, 72/11 ,,

PERKINS' H.P. terms can be varied to suit you!

FERGUSON TELEVISION MODEL 961T

12 in. TABLE MODEL FITTED WITH THE NEW NON-GLARE TINTED SCREEN.

£53-11-0 or on H.P.

£6-11-0 deposit & 14/3 weekly or 61/9 monthly
£13-11-0 ,, ,, 12/2 ,, ,, 52/8 ,,

FERGUSON MODEL 259A

FERGUSON 259A

A.C. SUPERHET

5 VALVE, 8 in. SPEAKER, PICK-UP AND SPEAKER SOCKETS. VERY GOOD TONE AND PERFORMANCE, WALNUT CABINET.

20 Guineas or on H.P. Terms

£2 deposit & 5/9 weekly or 24/11 monthly.
£5 ,, 4/10 ,, ,, 20/11 ,,
£8 ,, 3/11 ,, ,, 17/10 ,,

FERGUSON 941T

9 in. TUBE, 18 VALVE, FOR A.C. OR D.C.

BRILLIANT, STABLE PICTURE OF EXCELLENT PHOTOGRAPHIC QUALITY. A REALLY POPULAR AND RELIABLE SET. RECOMMENDED.

£47-11-6 or on H.P.

£5 deposit & 12/11 weekly or 56/0 monthly
£10 ,, 11/5 ,, ,, 49/6 ,,
£15 ,, 9/10 ,, ,, 42/7 ,,

ALL PRICES INCLUDE TAX

HIRE PURCHASE ORDERS DELIVERED IN A FEW HOURS.

NO FUSS, FORMALITY OR DELAY!

By September 1968, after extensive testing, the first production "Tipmaster", as it was to become known, was independently evaluated by engineers on behalf of *Motor Transport* and on 6 September a highly encouraging write-up appeared in that journal. A new company was formed, Perkins Commercial Services, to help promote the Tipmaster concept and demonstrator vehicles were sent across the country. The usefulness of the Tipmaster soon caught on and the vehicle became popular in many work areas from house building to local authority refuse collection. Today it is hard to imagine life without the Tipmaster workhorse. Over the years scores of customised Tipmasters have been built to accommodate different commercial needs and countless major vehicle manufacturers from Ford to Mercedes have included the Tipmaster and later tail-lift technologies on their various chassis. Although the Tipmaster turned out to be an international success for the Perkins group of companies, the current management have not rested on their laurels. Ian Terry and his team have spun off several other associated engineering companies as they have identified various market opportunities.

A Nissan Cabstar Tipper, one of the many different successful Tipmaster designs from the Perkins group of companies.

Ian Terry, Chairman & Managing Director of the Perkins Group outside the Dunmow, Essex motorcar showroom.

James Perkins would be immensely proud to know that his legacy of customer service and satisfaction is still safe in the hands of the present Perkins management and he would also be gratified to learn that the connection with the cycling fraternity is still as strong as ever. Ian Terry and his wife are members and supporters of James's old club, the Shaftesbury Cycling Club, and each year cyclists compete in a time-trial for the Perkins Trophy. In a changing commercial world where values of customer service seem to have disappeared, it is refreshing to find a Lea Valley company that is still maintaining the tradition of its founder, 120 years on.

REFERENCES

Author unknown, "Autobiographies of Motor cyclists – Perkins, James, Jun.", *The Motor Cycle*, 17 October, 1906.

Author unknown, "From Hand-Made Bicycles to Pantechnicons and Television", *Leyton Express & Independent*, Friday 20 January, 1961.

Lewis, Jim, *East Ham & West Ham Past*, Historical Publications, London, 2004.

Nichol, H., *The Shaftesbury Cycling Club, The First Hundred Years*, Shaftesbury Cycling Club, Essex, 1998.

Terry, Ian, *Perkins – A Century of Service*, Perkins Group, London, 1988.

Terry, Ian, Chairman and Managing Director of the Perkins Group, interview, October, 2007.

Note

Harry Terry, the man who had the vision to change, and probably save, the Perkins Group, died on 10 December 1982. He will be forever associated with the Tipmaster.

4. GILWELL PARK CHINGFORD – SPIRITUAL HOME OF THE SCOUT MOVEMENT

Gilwell Park is a 109-acre (44-hectare) site that nestles against the edge of Epping Forest and is located on high ground on the crest of the Lea Valley's eastern slopes overlooking the King George V reservoir. To millions of people who make up the Scout Movement across the world, Gilwell Park represents not just a campsite or a training centre where Scout Leaders come to prepare for their Wood Badge; it is their spiritual home.

Gilwell Park's recorded history goes back to the year 1407 when a John Crow owned the land, then known as Gyldiefords, which once formed part of the parish of Waltham Abbey, Essex. By 1422 Gyldiefords had been acquired by Richard Rolfe and the land became known as Gillrolfe's. The word 'Gill' is old English for glen and the remainder is the new owner's second name. At the time it was not unusual to identify land in this manner so that everyone would know to whom the plot belonged. In this particular example the land was clearly Rolfe's glen and he probably would have been known as Richard of Gill Rolfe.

After Rolfe's death, the land, probably about eight acres, remained with the family and was divided into two fields. The southerly field became known as Great Gilwell (the 'well' probably comes from the old English 'wella' meaning spring) while the northerly became Little Gilwell. Also at about this time it is thought that a wooden farmhouse stood on the spot where Gilwell Farm stands today. Around this time a Richard Osborne purchased 14 acres (5.6 hectares) of adjacent land and built a large property, which he called Osborne Hall.

Legend has it that Henry VIII once owned Gilwell and the surrounding land but there is no documentary evidence to support this claim. However, there are two possible reasons why some might have made a link been Henry VIII and Gilwell Park.

Gilwell had once been part of the parish of Waltham Abbey and it is known that Henry visited the Abbey on a number of occasions.

Queen Elizabeth's Hunting Lodge, Chingford is located on the southern edge of Chingford Plain. Originally called the "Great Standing", it was built for King Henry VIII in 1543.

He even considered making the Abbey Church a cathedral. This was before Waltham Abbey became the last monastic institution in England to succumb, in 1544, to Henry's dissolution of the monasteries.

Secondly, approximately one mile to the south of Gilwell Park is Queen Elizabeth's Hunting Lodge, thought to be the only remaining timber-framed building of its type still standing in Britain, if not the world. Although called Queen Elizabeth's Hunting Lodge it was actually built for Henry VIII in 1543. It was originally called the "Great Standing", probably because the upper floors were not enclosed (as they are today), allowing courtiers to stand as they watched the hunt or to fire their bows and arrows at passing deer. While it might disappoint local residents who like to claim a connection with early royal visitors to the area, there is no evidence to support the assertion that either Henry VIII or his daughter Queen Elizabeth I ever visited the Hunting Lodge.

Over the years Gilwell Park saw many different owners who, in general, increased the size of the estate. By the 1730s there appears to be an association with the notorious highwayman Dick Turpin. While it has never been claimed that Turpin was an owner, it has been suggested that Turpin lived on Gilwell land. This would seem highly unlikely, as he was a known fugitive with a price on his head. Such notoriety would hardly have allowed him the comfort of a permanent place of residence. Peter Rogers, the historian and writer of a booklet on Gilwell Park has uncovered convincing evidence, which suggests that Turpin was at least a visitor to the area. Rogers makes his case with the following argument "…on the far side of Gilwell Green stood a small group of wooden huts and cottages. These belonged to the estate workers of the neighbouring Lord of the Manor of Sewardstone and it was here that Turpin's young bride Ester Palmer lived and Turpin's son was born. This was probably as close a place as any that Turpin could call 'home'".

In 1754 William Skrimshire of Bow acquired both Great and Little Gilwell and he also bought half of Osborne's, which included the Hall. Peter Rogers has concluded that Skrimshire probably demolished the Hall and replaced it with another building also named Osborne Hall, which forms part of the present White House – now a conference centre. Timbers in the White House have been dated to this period.

The White House, now a reception area and conference centre, stands on the site of the earlier Osborne Hall. In the 1750s a later Osborne Hall was incorporated into the White House which, over the years, has been much modified.

The estate grew once more in 1771 when Leonard Tresilian, a warehouse owner from Brompton, Middlesex, became the new title-holder, adding more land, which brought the holding up to a total of 34 acres. Tresilian had builders add a wing to each side of Skrimshire's building and he also had extra rooms constructed at the back. By the early 1790s there were new owners of the house when William Bassett Chinnery and his wife Margaret, the daughter of the late Leonard Tresilian took up residence. Margaret had been left the Gilwell estate under the terms of her father's will.

One of the first acts of the Chinnerys was to change the name of Osborne Hall to Gilwell Hall and they then set about enlarging and beautifying the estate. Chinnery, a high ranking Treasury official and a shrewd man by all accounts, managed to acquire substantial parcels of adjacent land and over the years he also succeeded in obtaining more nearby land and evicted tenant farmers from their holdings. Margaret, in the meantime, took responsibility for redesigning the estate with formal gardens, a tree-lined walk, an archery lawn, a children's garden and an open-air theatre. As their social standing grew, lavish parties were held at Gilwell Hall that attracted not only the gentry and politicians but also members of the Royal Family. Visitors to the Hall were King George III and the Prince Regent, later to become King George IV. Adolphus Frederick, Duke of Cambridge, the King's seventh son became a great friend of the Chinnerys and stayed at the Hall as a guest, acting as tutor to their eldest son, George.

William Chinnery had done well for himself during his time at the Treasury, being promoted to Agent General for the Bahamas and other Colonies with an annual salary of over £4,000. His job had given him the responsibility for the payment of salaries and this would eventually lead him into temptation and bring about his downfall. Chinnery's lavish lifestyle had attracted the attention of the Prime Minister, Spencer Percival, who ordered officials to check certain accounting irregularities. On this occasion Chinnery was able to convince the investigators of his innocence and the matter was dropped. In early 1812, however, Captain Foveaux, a superintendent in New South Wales, wrote to the Prime Minister complaining about unpaid salaries. This time a more thorough investigation of Chinnery's accounts revealed that not only had he been misappropriating funds but he had also fraudulently claimed that pirates had attacked various ships to the Colonies. The investigation finally uncovered fraud totalling £81,000, a considerable amount of money by early-19th-century standards. On 17 March 1812, Chinnery was dismissed from his Treasury position and he quickly fled the country escaping to Gothenburg where he spent the rest of his life in exile. Had he remained in Britain he would no doubt have faced a long term in prison or more probably the hangman's noose.

On 25 March 1812 a debate was held in the House of Commons regarding the Exchequer's missing funds, which culminated in an order being issued to seize the Gilwell estate. This was a terrible blow to Margaret, the innocent party, who had lost her husband and now her home. If these events were not tragic enough, about three weeks after Chinnery's dismissal her daughter Caroline died

The statue of a bronze buffalo, presented by the Scouts of America in 1926, stands behinds the White House in an area called the Buffalo Lawn. In the background can be seen the stone balustrade that was once part of London Bridge.

at the age of 21. Now only George, the last of her three children remained, her youngest son Walter having died of typhoid at the age of 11 in 1802. Margaret left Gilwell and went to live in Manchester with her sister and, while there, she signed over the deeds of the Gilwell estate to the Exchequer. The Chinnerys' personal possessions were put up for sale and disposed of at public auction and later, in 1815, the estate was sold for £4,940.

The next owner of Gilwell was a Gilpin Gorst, the Deputy Governor of the Irish Society. In 1824, Gilpin's son Philip sold the property to Thomas Usborne who seems to have had an eye for history. During the replacement of the ageing London Bridge in 1826, Usborne managed to acquire some of the stone balustrades, which dated back to 1209. These he had transported to Gilwell and erected behind the Hall around the area that is known today as the Buffalo Lawn, so named after the gift of a Buffalo statue donated by the Boy Scouts of America in 1926.

Samuel Burgess became the next owner of Gilwell and during his time little seems to have happened regarding the estate's development. In 1858 William Alfred Gibbs, of Clapton, east London acquired the estate. People today may associate the name Gibbs with the familiar brand of toothpaste now manufactured by the Unilever Company. In fact it was William who came up with the formula for Gibbs Dentifrice toothpaste, a pink solid cake of abrasive paste that was sold in a round flat tin. It became popular with millions of consumers and is remembered by many who were

The Leopard Gates, which mark the main entrance to Gilwell Park, were designed and erected in 1928 by Don Potter, one of the Gilwell master craftsmen.

IMEDIATE OFFERS INVITED.   BY ORDER OF TRUSTEES.

Ideal Country Home for a City Man.

❧ CHINGFORD. ❧

About 1½ miles from the station, affording frequent and rapid access to the City, about 3 miles from Waltham Abbey Station, about 12 miles from London, and overlooking the well-known West Essex Golf Links.

Illustrated Particulars, Plan and Conditions of Sale

. OF A CHARMING OLD .

FREEHOLD RESIDENCE AND ESTATE

. KNOWN AS .

"Gillwell Park."

Situated as above, and comprising a **delightful Old-fashioned Family Residence** (containing 4 Reception-rooms, 10 Bedrooms, Bathroom, Servants' Rooms in Laundry, and good Domestic Offices), together with **Stabling for 6 horses**, Outbuildings, Farm-buildings, **beautifully wooded Grounds**, 2 Lodges, Orchard, and well-timbered Park-land, the whole lying in a ring fence and extending to an area of

SIXTY-EIGHT ACRES

(OR THEREABOUTS).

The bulk of the land is available for **immediate development as a Building Estate** if desired, without interfering with the privacy of the Residence, or otherwise depreciating its value.

Hunting 4 days a week. Golf close at hand.

Messieurs Tresidder & Co.

(In conjunction with Messrs. COCKETT & HENDERSON)

Have received instructions to Sell the above by Private Treaty, and if not so disposed of, by Auction, in one or more lots,

AT THE MART, TOKENHOUSE YARD, BANK OF ENGLAND, E.C.,

On Thursday, the 19th of July, 1906,

AT ONE O'CLOCK PRECISELY.

Copies of these Particulars with Plan, Views and Conditions of Sale, may be obtained at the Mart, E.C.; of the Solicitors, Messrs. GUSH, PHILLIPS, WALTERS & WILLIAMS, 3, Finsbury Circus, E.C.; of the Local Agents, Messrs. COCKETT & HENDERSON, 72, Bishopsgate Street Within, E.C., and of Station Gates, Woodford Green; or of the Auctioneers, Messrs. TRESIDDER & Co.,

Telegraphic Address:—"CORNISHERY, LONDON."
Telephone No.—4707 GERRARD.   13a, Cockspur Street, Pall Mall, London, S.W.

An advertisement for the sale of Gilwell Park in 1906. This would have been when the Gibbs family owned Gilwell. At the time the estate had become run down, although a prospective purchaser would not have appreciated this from the agent's description of the place.

children during the Second World War. The formula was applied to the teeth by first wetting a toothbrush then rubbing it on the paste's surface to charge the brush.

Sadly William Gibbs did not have sufficient funds to lavish on Gilwell and by the time of his death in 1900 the estate had fallen into disrepair. William's widow Sarah moved out of the Hall with her children and took up residence in two gardeners' cottages. Sarah died in 1905 and it is not clear who took care of her younger children although they seem to have left Gilwell around this time. However, Sarah's oldest son, Kenneth Yardley Gibbs remained and, in 1907, in an effort to raise capital, he sold eight acres of the northern end of Gilwell as the 'Gillwellbury estate. Kenneth then went to live at the farm until 1911 when this was sold to a local clergyman, the Reverend Cranshaw. The money raised from the sale would appear to have been a reasonable amount as Kenneth had a cottage built on the estate, presumably out of the proceeds, and it was here that he resided for the next ten years.

Robert Stephen Smyth Baden-Powell, 1st Baron Baden-Powell OM, GCMG, GCVQ, KCB (1857–1941), founder of the Scout Movement.

The 'Chief Scout.

To discover the next phase in Gilwell's history requires the reader to travel several thousand miles across the world to South Africa and to go back in time to the year 1896. Here, a remarkable man, Robert Baden-Powell, had been sent to support the British South Africa Company under siege in Bulawayo during the Second Matabele War. During his time there he frequently led reconnaissance operations into enemy territory and the skills he learned in tracking, camouflage and self-preservation would stand him in good stead for what he would accomplish later. Promoted to be the youngest colonel in the British Army, he returned to South Africa and, while carrying out his duties, he became trapped during the Second Boer War in the Siege of Mafeking. Under Baden-Powell's leadership as garrison commander the British troops, although totally outnumbered, withstood the siege for 217 days. The siege was finally lifted on 17 May

1900 when a British force, commanded by Colonel Mahon, fought their way into the town from the south.

On returning to England in 1903 Baden-Powell discovered that a military training manual that he had written, *Aids to Scouting*, had become a best-seller and was being used by youth groups. With encouragement from friends he decided to rewrite the manual to suit a younger audience. Always a practical man, in 1907 he took a group of 22 boys from mixed backgrounds to camp on Brownsea Island, Dorset to test various ideas from his book. No doubt the exercise was a success as the following year he published the now internationally famous *Scouting for Boys* that was first produced in six sections. The book is set out as a series of 26 'camp fire yarns', which are designed to inspire and encourage the reader while portraying a moral message.

Following the book's publication both girls and boys began forming Scout troops and the trend rapidly spread throughout the world.

Bottom left: Olave St Clair Soames (1889–1977) who became the wife of Baden-Powell in 1912. After progressing through the Girl Guide Movement she was appointed Chief Guide in 1918.

Bottom right: Percy Bantock Nevill (1887–1975), Commissioner for east London, was responsible for discovering Gilwell and recommending its purchase to the Scout Association.

In 1909 a Scout rally was held at Crystal Palace, London attended by both Boy and Girl Scouts. The following year the Girl Guides Movement was founded and Baden-Powell's sister, Agnes became Chief Guide. In 1912 Baden-Powell married Olave St Claire Soames and in 1918, after progressing through the Girl Guide Movement, she was appointed Chief Guide. The first World Scout Jamboree was held in Olympia, London in 1920 and Baden-Powell was acclaimed Chief Scout of the World.

The next chapter in the Gilwell story begins with the unlikely intervention of a wealthy Scottish publisher, William F. de Bois Maclaren who was also a Scout Commissioner from Rosneath, Dumbartonshire. About 1918, Maclaren was in the process of expanding his business to London when he approached Baden-Powell with an offer to fund the purchase of a campsite for the Scouts of east London. Initially a site at Ashdown Forest, Sussex was considered but it was soon realised that the distance Scouts would have to travel was unrealistic. Baden-Powell passed the matter to the Commissioner for east London, P. B. Nevill, who consulted Maclaren. Both men agreed that a more sensible area for a campsite would be Hainault Forest or Epping Forest and Maclaren agreed to put £7,000 towards the scheme. After a long search Nevill visited Gilwell Park, which was now in a sorry state of dilapidation. On contacting the estate agent he discovered that the asking price for the buildings

A picture of a group of Scouts in traditional uniforms probably taken in the 1930s. The boy second from the right has yet to acquire his uniform.

and 53 acres of land was £7,000, the exact amount that Maclaren had offered. Gilwell was purchased for the Scout Association in early 1919 and the official opening ceremony took place on Saturday 26 July 1919 when Mrs Maclaren cut the green and yellow ribbons that had been placed across the main gate.

In August 2007, the Scout Association celebrated its centenary with an International Jamboree at Hylands Park, Chelmsford, Essex, bringing together over 12,000 Scouts and Guides from 60 countries. The coverage of the event by television showed the world how young people of all nationalities can work, live and play together in peace, a fitting tribute to the movement's founder Baron Baden-Powell of Gilwell.

A statue of The Boy Scout, by Robert Tate McKenzie, presented to Gilwell Park by the Philadelphia Council Boy Scouts of America on 7 May 1966 as a mark of international brotherhood. The statue symbolises the "Ideal Scout".

Known as Big Mac, the clock tower is a memorial to Alfred Macintosh who was Camp Warden from 1945–1958. Affectionately known to many scouts as "Uncle Mac", he is probably best remembered for leading singsongs around the Gilwell campfire.

View from Gilwell Park across the Lea Valley. The large expanse of water is the King George V Reservoir.

REFERENCES

Baden-Powell, Robert, *Scouting for Boys*, The Scout Association, London, 1997.

Begbie, Harold, *The Story of Baden-Powell: The Wolf That Never Sleeps,* Hodder & Stoughton, London, 1918.

Higgs, Eric & Bascombe, Ken, *Waltham Abbey*, Pitkin Pictorials Ltd., Andover, Hampshire, 1995.

Kiernan, R.H., *Baden-Powell*, Harrap Publishing, London, 1939.

Rogers, Peter, *Gilwell Park – A Brief History and Guided Tour*, The Scout Association, Gilwell, 1998.

Note

At the fifth World Scout Jamboree in 1937, Baden-Powell announced his retirement, at the age of 80, from public Scouting life. Five years before he had written a foreword to his book *Scouting for Boys*. Although the style and choice of words, as might be expected, are dated it is worthwhile reproducing the first three paragraphs here to allow the reader a glimpse of his thoughts.

I WAS A BOY ONCE.

The best time I had as a boy was when I went about as a sea scout with my four brothers on the sea round the coasts of England. Not that we were real Sea Scouts, because Sea Scouts weren't invented in those days. But we had a sailing boat of our own on which we lived and cruised about, at all seasons and in all weathers, and we had a jolly good time – taking the rough with the smooth.

Then in my spare time as a schoolboy I did a good lot of scouting in the woods in the way of catching rabbits and cooking them, observing birds and tracking animals, and so on. Later on, when I got into the Army, I had endless fun big-game hunting in the jungles in India and Africa and living among the backwoodsmen in Canada. Then I got real scouting in South African campaigns.

Well, I enjoyed all this kind of life so much that I thought "Why should not boys at home get some taste of it too". I knew that every true red-blooded boy is keen for adventure and open-air life, and so I wrote this book to show how it could be done.

5. HIGH BEECH – BIRTHPLACE OF BRITISH MOTORCYCLE SPEEDWAY RACING

The period following the Great War was a time when the nation's conservative attitudes changed dramatically. People, particularly during the 1920s, began letting their hair down as they sought new pleasures and looked for thrills and excitement as they tried to put the horrors of the war years behind them. Energetic dances like the Charleston became popular and the three-four time of the waltz appeared decidedly sedate to those young things on an enjoyment mission. Jazz music became all the rage and even the movies that were once silent got a new lease of life when Al Jolson starred in the first talking picture to be released, *The Jazz Singer.*

With the public's seemingly insatiable quest for things new and exciting, it would appear that the most unlikely place for the thrill seekers to congregate was at the highest point of the Lea Valley's eastern slopes, in Epping Forest, behind the King's Oak Hotel at High Beech, Essex. Here however, on Sunday 19 February 1928 the crowds flocked in their thousands to see the first official motorcycle speedway race (referred to as speedway) to be staged on British soil.

The King's Oak Hotel, High Beech, Essex. Behind this building on a dirt track in Epping Forest, Britain's first speedway meeting took place on 19 February 1928.

In Britain there are at least two other places which claim to be the first to stage a speedway meeting. One was at Camberley, Surrey on 7 May 1927 when riders went round a dirt track in a clockwise direction, not the conventional anti-clockwise direction, and another in the same year for a meeting at Droylsden, Manchester, which was ridden the conventional way around the track. Perhaps the best way to judge if a meeting satisfies the criteria of being first is if it is recognised by an official sanctioning body. In the case of High Beech the Auto-Cycle Union (ACU) was the official licensing body in Britain for the sport. The former two claims were not sanctioned.

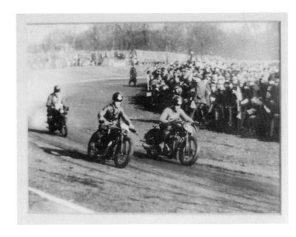

A photograph that hangs on the wall of the King's Oak Hotel showing speedway riders competing at an early meeting at High Beech.

There is an ongoing debate as to which country hosted the first speedway meeting with Australia and America vying for pole position. On 17 December 1923, the Australian newspaper the *Maitland Mercury* reported that the first meeting took place at the Maitland Showground in the Lower Hunter Valley, New South Wales on 15 December that year. However, both Australia and America have claims of earlier meetings with the Americans asserting that one of their riders, Don Johns, was broadsiding (a controlled slide at speed around a bend on a dirt track) before 1914. By the time of High Beech's opening the sport had already developed a sizeable following in Australia and experienced riders started coming to Britain.

Jack Hill-Bailey, a railway engineer and Secretary of the Ilford Motor Cycle Club, had met officials of the ACU at High Beech in January 1928 and, after an inspection of the track that lasted about three hours, a permit was granted to hold a speedway meeting, providing that certain conditions were met. These were that each rider should wear a crash helmet for safety and that all those attending speedway events must be club members. The latter would seem a difficult challenge to meet, given the timing of the first meeting, but Hill-Bailey had somehow managed to persuade the Daily Mirror to run an article on the forthcoming speedway event and applications for membership soon came flooding in.

On the morning of 19 February 1928, Hill-Bailey and his wife Kay left their home at 41 Hicking Road, Ilford on Jack's 1,000cc Harley Davidson combination. Kay had packed herself into the sidecar along with 2,000 tickets and 500 programmes that were intended for sale at the first official dirt track meeting to be staged in Britain.

A programme announcing the 39th meeting at Lea Bridge Speedway, Saturday 3 August 1929.

The front cover of *Speedway News* (21 April 1934) showing a rider's leg trailing.

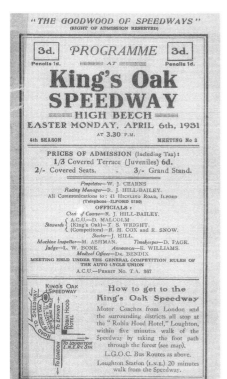

A 1939 Rye House Speedway programme. Rye House, founded in 1936, was recently re-formed and is the only speedway club surviving in the Lea Valley.

A 1931 High Beech Speedway programme that advertises covered seats and a grandstand. It should also be noted that buses and coaches terminated at the Robin Hood Hotel on the Epping Road and spectators were invited to walk to the meeting through the forest. This was to prevent congestion on the roads leading to High Beech.

When Hill-Bailey and his wife arrived at High Beech at around 8am, some two and a half hours before the meeting was due to start, they were surrounded by a crowd of about 2,000 people who had gathered outside the Kings Oak Hotel. The Hill-Baileys must have felt under siege from the crowd whose early presence was quite unexpected. When Jack and his committee had met to discuss expected spectator numbers they had worked on the basis that if 3,000 people turned up on the day they would be doing extremely well. At a makeshift entrance booth made out of boxes Kay sold all of the 2,000 tickets and 500 programmes within an hour and a half of arriving. The tickets were sold for sixpence (2.5p) and the programmes for twopence (0.83p). With half an hour to go before the start of the meeting it was claimed that 15,000 people were inside the ground and thousands more were streaming along the roads leading to the Royal Oak. By the time racing started it was estimated that around 30,000 people had arrived.

One can imagine that the organisers of the event must have felt completely overwhelmed by the masses of excited people who had turned up, some late and probably in a state of frustration due to delays caused by the crowds blocking the roads to High Beech. To get a flavour of the atmosphere on that day it is worth recording what Jack Hill-Bailey wrote:

> The governing body had insisted that all spectators were to be kept behind the rope barrier inside the track. It soon became obvious that there was little chance of anyone observing this rule and, in fact, the racing was actually carried out between two closely packed lines of spectators. Frankly, the whole meeting was a nightmare for every one of the officials. We expected every moment to see some daring rider lose control of his machine and crash into the crowd, but I am thankful to say that actually there was no accident of any kind.

Perhaps the occasion is best summed up when Hill-Bailey remarked, "What right had 30,000 people to cram into a ground which had accommodation for a mere 2,000?"

The four following rules had been printed in the programme, which the ACU expected the spectators to obey, followed by a stern warning. These were:

> Spectators must keep to the inner portion of the track behind ropes.
> No dogs allowed inside under any conditions.

Spectators will only be allowed to cross the track between events and at one place only.

If competitors fall they must be left to the Marshals. On no account must the public invade the track.

These rules are laid down by the Governing Body, the Auto-Cycle Union and unless strictly adhered to the Stewards of the Meeting have power to stop this event and other future events.

Chaotic conditions apart, with people climbing surrounding trees and telegraph poles to get a view and other spectators massing on the centre of the track, the meeting was a resounding success. One enthusiastic customer wrote to the local newspaper congratulating the club on the cheapness of the sixpence entrance fee, which he calculated to be "50 thrills for one penny". Two Australian riders, Billy Galloway and Keith Mackay, had taken part in the meeting but it seems that the track, formerly an abandoned cycle circuit roundish in shape, was not to their liking. These two riders were experienced leg-trailers and it would seem that only one bend had a loose cinder surface where they could demonstrate their broadsiding skills. The rest of the riders were British and had not competed on dirt tracks before. Many were riding everyday motorcycles of differing engine capacities that had not been stripped of lamps, speedometers and horns.

The team picture of the High Beech Speedway taken in 1930. From left to right: Jack Hill-Bailey, Fred Law, Phil Bishop, George Bishop, Jack Barnett, Syd Edmonds, Stan Baines and Charlie King.

High Beech hero Phil Bishop (centre) after winning the Cearns Gold Cup, by beating the Australian rider Vic Huxley (left) and his local team mate Syd Edmonds (right). On the left of the picture is Jack Hill-Bailey and the man in the smart suit and hat is the promoter and donor of the trophy, W.J. Cearns.

A photograph of the Lea Bridge Speedway team taken in 1930. The rider in the centre, presumably the captain, is sitting on a Sunbeam motorcycle.

Photograph taken at Lea Bridge in the 1930s. On the left and holding two cups is Frank Arthur, on the right is the Australian rider Max Grosskreutz. In the white coat is Mr E. Bass, the meeting promoter. Others in the picture are not known.

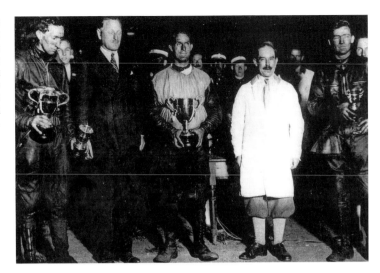

Walthamstow Wolves' first post-war speedway meeting, Monday 4 April 1949. The rider on the front of the programme is drawn wearing the Wolves team logo.

OFFICIAL 6D PROGRAMME

Walthamstow STADIUM SPEEDWAY

FIRST MEETING, MONDAY, 4th APRIL 1949, AT 7.30 p.m.
NATIONAL LEAGUE MATCH (Division II)
WALTHAMSTOW v SOUTHAMPTON
Held under the Regulations of the Speedway Control Board.
Track Licence No. 16/49.   Permit No. SP. 478.   Track Length—382 yards
BETTING STRICTLY PROHIBITED

Nevertheless, despite all the early problems experienced by the organisers, the sport of speedway had got off to a flying start at High Beech and quickly spread to major towns and cities through the country and also into Europe. New tracks, including High Beech, were built with safety barriers and crowd control fencing, loose cinder and shale surfaces became the norm, riders' clothing improved and became more protective and new regulations ensured that track bikes were built to a standard with engine sizes limited to 500cc, and gearboxes and brakes were omitted. Towns and cities with speedway tracks developed teams who rode in leathers with slipover racing jackets emblazoned with distinguishing team logos. National leagues were formed and there was considerable rivalry between clubs, much like football today.

A number of speedway teams sprung up in the Lea Valley. These were: Rye House, Walthamstow, Lea Bridge, Harringay, Hackney Wick and West Ham. However, over the years the sport declined and the only speedway club that survives in the Lea Valley is Rye House (founded in 1936), which currently runs two teams, the Rye House Rockets and the Rye House Cobras (formerly the Raiders). The site of the former Harringay stadium now houses a superstore; the West Ham track and the surrounding area is a housing estate; the Lea Bridge track is a light industrial complex; Walthamstow Stadium, which up until recently was still in the ownership of the original Chandler family and hosted regular greyhound meetings, has been sold to a developer and greyhound racing has ceased.

It is currently planned that the grounds of the former Hackney Wick Stadium will feature in the 2012 Olympics where it is possible that a cycle velodrome will be built. Should this plan materialise, the author would like to take this opportunity to encourage the authorities to erect a plaque on the new Olympic building as a reminder to later generations that another kind of popular sport with a very large fan base, speedway racing, once occupied the place.

Walthamstow Stadium, home of the Walthamstow Wolves Speedway team 1934–1935 and 1949–1951.

The entrance to the Speedway Museum, Paradise Wildlife Park, Broxbourne, Hertfordshire

The top bend of the Walthamstow speedway track still in place (2007) sandwiched between the greyhound track and the centre grass area.

REFERENCES

Author unknown, "Speedway Returns to its Birthplace", *Walthamstow Guardian*, London, 26 February, 2004.

Baker, T.F.T. (ed.), *The Victoria County History: Middlesex*, Vol. 10, Institute of Historical Research, University of London, 1995.

Bamford, Robert, *Homes of British Speedway*, NPI Media Group, United Kingdom, 2001.

Bondy, Mike, "Speedway at the Stow", *Walthamstow Guardian*, London, 30 October 2003.

Chaplin, John, *A Fistful of Twist Grip*, Penrove Books, London, 1995.

Fenn, Chris, *Hackney Speedway: Friday at Eight*, Tempus Publishing Ltd., Gloucestershire, 2003.

Jacobs, Norman, *Speedway in London*, Tempus Publishing Ltd., Gloucestershire, 2001.

Lewis, Jim, *East Ham & West Ham Past*, Historical Publications, London, 2004.

Stone, Terry, a former speedway rider with Rayleigh Rockets and now a volunteer with the Speedway Museum, Paradise Wildlife Park, White Stubbs Lane, Broxbourne, Hertfordshire EN10 7QA, (a personal conversation, August 2007).

Wynn, Paul, media and public relations department Walthamstow Stadium, London E17, (a personal conversation, August 2007).

Note 1

Constructed in 1932, Hackney Wick Stadium, Waterden Road, Hackney Wick was originally built for greyhound racing. In 1935 a Speedway racing circuit was opened and a team known as the Hackney Wick Wolves raced there until the outbreak of the Second World War in 1939. Speedway did not resume at Hackney Wick at the cessation of hostilities, but in 1963 a new track was opened on the site. The team was named the Hackney Hawks and rode at the venue until 1983. In 1984 the team name changed to the Hackney Kestrels and they rode at the stadium until 1990. The old stadium was demolished and between 1994 and 1995 a new stadium and track was built. In 1995 and 1996 the stadium hosted the British Speedway Grand Prix. A team called the London Lions rode at the stadium in 1996 but their tenure was short lived as the owners ran into financial difficulties and went bankrupt.

Note 2

Walthamstow Stadium in Chingford Road, Walthamstow opened in 1933 for greyhound racing and in 1934 Speedway racing was introduced but seems to have only lasted for one season. The team was called Walthamstow Wolves. In 1935 Hackney Wick Wolves began racing at Hackney Wick Stadium, Waterden Road, Hackney Wick and it would appear that the Walthamstow team transferred there. While more research is required to confirm this point the team name, Hackney Wick Wolves, does not roll off the tongue too easily. On Monday 17 October 1949 Speedway racing resumed at Walthamstow (racing at Hackney Wick by a team called the Hawks did not restart until 1963) when the Wolves, a National League Second Division club, took on the National Trophy champions, Belle Vue Aces, in a special challenge match. The Wolves won a closely fought victory, 43 points to their opponents' 40. Speedway racing ended at Walthamstow by the close of the 1951 season mainly due to a combination of falling gate receipts and complaints of noise from local residents.

Note 3

Lea Bridge Stadium was once situated at the eastern end of what is now Rigg Approach, Leyton (Waltham Forest). The stadium was built in 1929 and speedway racing continued up to the time of the Second World War. Clapton Orient Football Club moved from their ground in Homerton (now part of Hackney) in 1930 to the Lea Bridge Stadium. The club remained there until 1937 when they left to go to a new ground in Brisbane Road, Leyton. Here, the club adopted the now more familiar name of Leyton Orient.

Note 4

The author would like to thank Terry Stone of the Speedway Museum, Broxbourne for generously lending his personal collection of historic speedway photographs and other memorabilia, which has helped considerably in the production of this chapter.

6. AN 18TH-CENTURY LEA VALLEY LIFT OFF

The Lea Valley has been the scene of a number of pioneering developments that have led to important breakthroughs in aeronautical science. Names such as Alliott Verdon Roe, Sir George Edwards and Sir Geoffrey de Havilland have strong associations with the region. In their time these men made major contributions to the evolving technology of aviation, influencing the work of local, national and international manufacturers. Occasionally when researching local developments in aviation history a story is uncovered that has to be told.

It was Leonardo da Vinci (1452–1519) who appears to have been the first to make a serious attempt to study flight scientifically. We know from his writings that he believed a bird was no more than a type of apparatus that worked according to the laws of mathematics. He reasoned that man was capable of building an exact copy, with the exception of the bird's muscle power. Therefore, he concluded that by replacing the bird's muscle power with that of a man, a flying machine could become a practical proposition. We know that da Vinci must have considered the possibility of flight and flying machines for some time as is evidenced by his writing and the large quantity of drawings that he left behind on the subject. His bequest has given later generations the opportunity to study and test his ideas. Physically recreating some of da Vinci's flying machine ideas has enabled scientists and engineers to appreciate how far advanced his thinking was.

Although it is not absolutely clear, the next phase in the history of flight could have occurred on 8 August 1709. It has been claimed, but apparently not officially recorded, that a Brazilian priest, Father Bartholomeu Lourenco Gusmao, successfully demonstrated indoors in Lisbon, before King John V of Portugal, what was probably a type of hot-air balloon. However, it was not until the year 1783 that man succeeded in doing what his ancestors had only dreamed of; defying gravity and leaving the ground. The method of achieving this was probably not quite what Leonardo da Vinci had envisaged.

The Montgolfier brothers, Michel and Jacques, have been credited with the first public demonstration, on 4 June 1783, of a hot-air balloon rising into the atmosphere. This was achieved in their hometown of Annonay, France, although they claimed to have privately tested a model the year before. Like several early experimenters the brothers were relatively wealthy, their money coming from a paper-manufacturing business. It is possible that the technology employed in their paper-making business had helped them to construct the balloon, which was made by lining a large hessian bag, about 35 feet across (10.7 metres), with paper. The balloon was reported to have risen to a height of 3,000 feet (915 metres), and travelled a distance of over one and a half miles (2.4 km). The Montgolfiers had used a lighted straw-filled burner suspended beneath the balloon to give it lift. On landing the flaming basket somehow came into contact with the balloon's fabric and the envelope was destroyed.

The next experiment by the brothers was considerably more ambitious and was performed at Versailles on 19 September 1783 before King Louis XVI and Marie Antoinette. This time the balloon had passengers in a basket slung beneath; a sheep, a duck and a cockerel. Animals were chosen to see if they could survive in the atmosphere above ground level. Unfortunately the balloon's fabric, which had now been improved by waterproofing, was torn at launch and the flight lasted only about eight minutes returning to earth around two miles from the point of take-off. The sheep and the duck returned unharmed but the cockerel had sustained an injury. Apparently someone suggested that the injury was due to the harmful effects of the rarefied atmosphere. However, it was later concluded that the sheep had probably trodden on the cockerel.

The relative success of the flight of the animals gave the Montgolfiers the confidence to build a larger balloon for the purpose of carrying people. This new design would carry two people who would have to stand opposite each other, as a balanced payload, on a circular platform suspended by ropes below the balloon's canopy. To create the hot air for lifting the balloon a straw-burning fire-basket was hung from chains inside the canopy and this could be serviced by the aeronauts through holes cut into either side of the balloon's fabric. Francois Pilatre de Rozier, a chemist and physicist who, on occasions, was accompanied by guests, made the first tethered flights. On 15 October 1783, he ascended to a height of 324 feet (99 metres). As the ascents were deemed successful the first free flight was made by de Rozier and the Marquis d'Arlandes and took place on 21 November 1783, from the Bois de Boulogne, Paris. The balloon stayed aloft for approximately 25 minutes and reached a reported height of around 1,500 feet (457 metres) – some reports claim double this height – finally returning to earth around six miles (10km) away from the starting point. Apparently de Rozier and his crewmate were extremely lucky to return safely as during the flight the platform on which they were standing began to break up.

In parallel with the hot-air balloon flights of the Montgolfier brothers, others had been experimenting with a different lifting medium; hydrogen. Interestingly, it was the discoveries of the eccentric and somewhat reclusive English scientist, Henry Cavendish (1731–1810) that made these flights possible. Coincidentally Cavendish was born in France at Nice where his parents, Lady Anne Gray, the daughter of the Duke of Kent and Lord Charles Cavendish, the son of the second Duke of Devonshire, were staying. On returning to England, young Henry, at the age of 11, was sent to the school of Doctor Newcome in Hackney, east London. At 18 he went to St. Peter's College, Cambridge but left when he was 22 without graduating. In 1766, 13 years later, he published his first paper entitled "On Factious Airs". The discovery of what Cavendish termed "inflammable air" was later named hydrogen by the French scientist Antoine Lavoisier.

After making a successful test flight with a model, Professor Jacques Alexandre Cesar Charles built a full-size hydrogen balloon that was different in construction from the hot-air variety. The balloon's envelope was some 26 feet (7.9 metres) in diameter and made from fabric coated with a rubbery adhesive. Around the balloon's middle was a wooden ring. Attached to the ring was netting, which completely surrounded the top half of the balloon and suspended from the ring was the passenger basket. Two valves were fitted to the balloon's envelope, one at the top and the other at the bottom. The latter allowed the balloon to be inflated by connecting it to the hydrogen source. Once airborne, either valve could be operated to release gas, not just to descend. This was to ensure that the balloon's envelope was kept fully under control, particularly if the fabric began to expand dangerously due to sunlight warming the hydrogen inside or when the external air pressure fell, and expansion again occurred, as the balloon gained height.

On 1 December 1783, Charles and a companion, reported to be one of the Robert brothers who had helped make the balloon, took off from the Tuileries Gardens, Paris. On board they had stowed a quantity of food, a thermometer, a barometer, warm clothing and sandbags to use as ballast. A little over two hours later they landed, without a hitch, at the town of Nesles after travelling a distance of around 27 miles (42km). Although it was late in the day and getting dark, Charles ascended once more, this time on his own, as he wanted to observe the sunset. Less than a year after Charles's first successful flight in a hydrogen balloon, one of those remarkable Lea Valley firsts took place in England.

Vincenzo Lunardi (1759–1806), a clerk at the Neapolitan Embassy in London, and later to become Secretary to Prince Caramanico, the Neapolitan Ambassador, was by all accounts a handsome ladies' man and showman. Inspired by two unmanned experimental balloon flights by his fellow countryman Count Zambeccari, in England in November 1783, he began a subscription scheme, in July 1784, to raise money to fund a hydrogen balloon flight, also in England. By the middle of August that year the construction of his balloon was complete. Then in true showman style Lunardi arranged to have the envelope inflated with air and the balloon hung from the ceiling in the hall of London's Pantheon (the building once stood on the south side of Oxford Street) for all to admire. It has been suggested that Lunardi had the idea that in trying to make the first successful balloon flight in England, his reputation with the ladies would be enhanced. The flight was scheduled to take off from the grounds of London's Royal Chelsea Hospital. However, after two failed attempts before him by others, when the hot-air balloon caught fire, all flights from the Hospital grounds were cancelled.

Lunardi approached the commander of the Honourable Artillery Company, Sir Watkin Lewis, and after protracted negotiations it was agreed that he could take off from the Company's training ground

A stone commemorating the first flight in England (15 September 1784) by the Italian balloonist Vincenzo Lunardi, placed near to where he landed at Welham Green, Hertfordshire. The locals refer to the area as balloon corner.

A modern road sign at Welham Green, near to where Vincenzo Lunardi landed, keeps alive the memory of this early Lea Valley aeronaut.

at Moorfields, London. At approximately1pm on 15 September 1784, before a crowd of around150,000 (some estimates suggest figures of anything from100,000 to 200,000), which included many dignitaries such as the Prince of Wales, Lord North and the Duchess of Devonshire, he ascended to what must have been a considerable height as the sight of the balloon envelope from the ground was said to be about the size of a tennis ball. Apart from food and wine, no doubt to sustain him on his journey, it is reported that Lunardi took three passengers with him. These were his pet cat and dog and a caged pigeon.

After drifting in a northerly direction for some time he came down in a field at Welham Green, Hertfordshire, where it is claimed he discharged ballast by placing his dog and cat in the care of a woman (no mention of what happened to the caged pigeon) then once more ascended. His next return to earth was at the small hamlet of Standon Green End in Hertfordshire, just north of Ware. On

After Lunardi deposited his dog and his cat at Welham Green he took off once again heading north up the Lea Valley. He descended for the second time, landing in a field at Standon End, Hertfordshire. The stone with its protective railing marks the spot.

Lunardi's balloon, inflated with air, hanging from the ceiling in the hall of London's Pantheon.

descending, he threw out his mooring rope so that labourers from the nearby Knoll Farm, working in the field below, could catch and assist his landing. Apparently, on seeing such an apparatus descending from the sky the men ran off in fear. The present owner of the farmhouse told the author that it was the women of the farm, on hearing the shouts of the labourers as they fled in panic, who went outside to see what all the commotion was about and assisted Lunardi with the landing by catching hold of the mooring rope. It is recorded that the flight from Moorfields took around two hours and 15 minutes.

In the field where the balloon landed stands a large stone surrounded by protective iron railings. This monument is referred to locally as the 'balloon stone'. Apparently the original stone was stolen, presumably for building material, and Arthur Giles Puller, the then owner of Knoll Farm, replaced it with another in November 1875. The farm was then part of the Youngsbury estate. On top of the 'balloon stone' is a hinged copper plate inscribed with these words taken from the original inscription:

> *Let posterity know*
> *And knowingly be astonished*
> *That*
> *On the 15th day of September 1784*
> *Vincent Lunardi of Lucca Tuscany*
> *The first aerial traveller in Britain*
> *Mounting from the Artillery ground*
> *In London*
> *And*
> *Traversing the regions of the air*
> *For two hours and fifteen minutes*

In this spot
Revisited the Earth
On this rude monument
For ages be recorded
That wondrous enterprise
Successfully achieved
By the powers of chemistry
And the fortitude of man
That improvement in science
Which

The great author of all knowledge

Patronising by his providence
The inventions of mankind
Hath generously permitted
To their benefit
His own eternal glory

There is also a monument at Welham Green, the site where Lunardi first landed, although not quite so grand as that erected at Standon Green End. The monument is placed on the grass verge at the junction of two roads and is known by some local residents as 'balloon corner'. Approximately 150 metres south of this spot is a further dedication to the Lea Valley aeronaut in the name of

Bottom left: Vincenzo Lunardi ascending from the grounds of the Honourable Artillery Company, Moorfields, London on 15 September 1784.

Bottom right: Vincenzo Lunardi was known for his showmanship and this is evidenced by the union flag decoration on his second balloon.

Vincenzo Close, now part of a modern housing estate. This particular site would have once been open ground and probably a field close to where Lunardi came down.

While it seems certain that Lunardi was the first to fly in England, other claims that he was the first to fly in Britain are not true. Just over two weeks before Lunardi ascended from Moorfields, the Scot, James Tytler (1747–1805) made his ascent to a height of 350 feet (106 metres), in a hot-air balloon, from Comley Gardens, Edinburgh on 27 August 1784. Always a showman, Lunardi decorated the envelope of one of his balloons with the Union Flag and made many more flights in England and Scotland and later on the Continent. Although it cannot be claimed that Lunardi's flights were purely in the interests of science, he did however make an early contribution to the overall knowledge of aeronautics. Had the wind on 15 September 1784 not been blowing from a southerly direction, it would not have been possible for the author to claim Lunardi's flight as another Lea Valley first!

An engraving of Vincenzo Lunardi, paddling across the River Thames, while demonstrating his invention for saving people from drowning!

A painting depicting the large crowds that Vincenzo Lunardi attracted each time he made a balloon ascent. The poles to the left of the picture were to hold the balloon while it was being inflated.

An early map showing Moor Fields adjacent to London Wall.

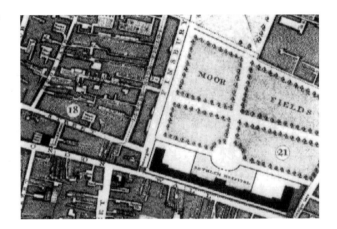

REFERENCES

Carter, David, Interview at Knoll Farm, Standon Green End, Hertfordshire, June 2007.

Dale, Henry, *Early Flying Machines*, The British Library, London, 1992.

Owen, David, *Lighter Than Air*, The Apple Press, London, 1999.

Skilton, David, *Balloon Ascents*, University of Cardiff.

Slyfield, Bryan, *The Day Count Zambeccari Dropped In*, The Horsham Society, Horsham, April 2007.

Stephen, Leslie & Lee Sidney (eds.), *Dictionary of National Biography*, Vol.X11, Oxford University Press, 1917.

Stephen, Leslie & Lee Sidney (eds.), *Dictionary of National Biography*, Vol.X1X, Oxford University Press, 1917.

7. THE ABSOLUTELY INCREDIBLE HARPER TWELVETREES

It is not often, from the distance of the 21st century that we are allowed the opportunity to look inside the mind of a 19th-century entrepreneur, industrialist and philanthropist. This man, Harper Twelvetrees, through his energy, thoughtfulness and morality, has set an example which many of us would find hard to follow. Taking account of the time, the examples he set, although quite revolutionary, may not exactly match our present expected standards of equality. However, some of his initiatives would do credit to many government agencies and employers if they were introduced today. While carrying out research for this chapter I was particularly fortunate in discovering a file of correspondence which has allowed a unique glimpse of a mid-19th-century industrial area in the southern part of the Lea Valley.

Harper Twelvetrees
(1823–1881).

Harper Twelvetrees was born at Biggleswade in Bedfordshire in December 1823, the son of a local builder. At the age of 14 he was apprenticed in a neighbouring town to the printing, stationery and bookselling trade. When he was only 16 the owner of the firm for which he was working died and Harper was asked to take over the management of the business. For agreeing to this, he was given a share in the firm. While, on the face of it, this seemingly rash decision by the inheritors of the business may have been no more than an expedient, it does show that in a little over two years young Harper had mastered the requisite skills to cope with the task before him. It also suggests that he was considered trustworthy.

Harper stayed with the firm until he was 22 and while there he took the opportunity to educate himself. He would get up early in the morning and spend the time between

3.30am and 5.30am reading and studying. The subjects he studied were wide ranging and covered English literature, ancient and modern history, chemistry and, as he put it, 'several of the sciences'. It would seem that he had also deliberately tried to strengthen this knowledge by giving lectures to various temperance societies and mechanics institutes. By 1845, Harper appears to have set up business on his own account in another part of Bedfordshire and it was during this time that his interest in chemistry deepened; this subject was to have a major influence on his later life.

In 1848 Harper moved to London and went into partnership with the idea of manufacturing a cheap range of products for laundry use, but he soon gave up on the venture. This, he said was because "…the vexatious regulations of the excise in connection with the soap-duties interfered with the full development of that particular branch to which my attention had been directed". A little while after the move, in 1849, Harper's wife Mary died.

In 1851 Harper married Isabella Noble and soon afterwards he received a proposal from his father-in-law, John Noble, then Mayor of Boston in Lincolnshire who, at the time, ran a printing and bookselling business with his son in Market Place. John Noble had wished to retire from the business and he invited Harper to enter into partnership with his son. This Harper did and the partnership lasted four years. In 1853 the duty on soap, which had earlier caused Harper to abandon his manufacturing aspirations, was abolished. Now, Harper had the encouragement he needed to re-evaluate his earlier plans to set up as a manufacturer of cheap laundry products; only this time he was determined to go it alone.

In about 1855, Harper Twelvetrees with his second wife, Isabella and young son Walter moved from Boston and took up residence at Tudor Grove, Hackney in east London. Shortly afterwards Harper started to manufacture his laundry products at a factory in Goswell Road in the neighbouring borough of Islington. In 1858 Harper moved his business to a larger factory site adjacent to the River Lea in Three Mills Lane at Bromley-by-Bow. As there was living accommodation within the factory complex Harper moved his family onto the site. The house was a detached building having a basement and three storeys; each floor had four rooms. There was a garden of about four acres and also a paddock of similar size. Previously the house was said to have been the home of a refugee Huguenot family named Lefevre. It was also said that the house was the birthplace of Shaw-Lefevre (the family name may have been changed to avoid persecution) who later became Speaker of the House of Commons. Shaw-Lefevre (1794–1888), on his retirement

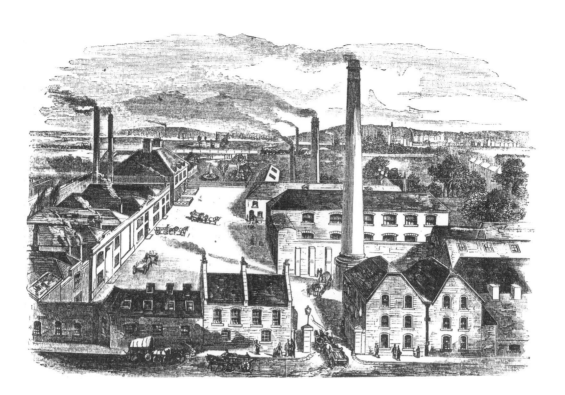

An engraving of Harper Twelvetrees' Imperial Chemical Works in Three Mills Lane, Bromley-by-Bow. Although the scene depicted is c.1860, a number of buildings on the site pre-date this time. Note the elevated railway line in the background, which today still follows the same east-west route. On the left of the picture, masts of sailing barges can just be made out on the adjacent Lee Navigation.

as Speaker, was raised to the peerage under the title of Viscount Eversley of Heckford. When Harper moved in to his new residence he decided to name the property, 'Eversley House' after its former tenant.

We are extremely fortunate to have Walter Noble Twelvetrees' (1852-1941) childhood recollections of the house and its surroundings recorded in correspondence in 1932, when he was 80. Walter recalls that the house:

> "...was evidently old, as all the rooms etc. were panelled. I presume the house stood long ago in the middle of the whole area later occupied by the works and grounds, and may have been a farm house with land extending towards Poplar, long before the railway was built."

The River Lea also appears to have made a lasting impression on Walter when he wrote "during high spring tides, the gardens of Eversley House were sometimes completely flooded, within a few ft. of the house and I have seen 2 or 3ft. of water in the basement." He also tells us that he did not know when the works were built. However, he explained "I remember that the various buildings looked old when I first saw them in 1859 or 1860." We again learn from his letters that:

> "... before 1860, there were three factories to which entrance
> was gained through the work's gateway. One of these formed
> the nucleus of Imperial Works [Harper Twelvetrees
> Manufactory], another was occupied by Messrs. Cleugh, jute
> manufacturers and the third by Messrs. Hayter, who carried on
> some process connected with woolly substances, probably the
> production of shoddy."

Shoddy was a fibre made from old cloth and the name has passed
into modern language and now refers to anything of poor quality.
The railway referred to by Walter formed the southern boundary of
the site and was the London Tilbury and Southend line, which
crossed the River Lea at the same point as the railway does today.

It should be remembered that at the time thousands of people were
dying in London of cholera and typhoid and this had provoked a
massive programme to build new sewers and to improve the
capital's supply of drinking water. Coincidentally, the Abbey Mills
pumping station at Stratford, completed in 1868, was located
approximately 500 metres to the east of Harper's Imperial
Chemical Works. The building was jointly designed by Sir Joseph
Bazalgette (an Enfield-born man) and Edmund Cooper, and formed
part of Bazalgette's new London sewage system. Interestingly, when
Walter Noble Twelvetrees recalled his early childhood memories of
Bromley-by-Bow (in 1932) he wrote that he remembered the
ground to the north of Three Mills Lane was situated behind a long
wall that ran the length of the lane and was known as "Farmer
Mann's". He further recalled that when the Metropolitan Drainage
Works were in progress that there was "excavating, tunnelling or
boring operations in Mann's fields". It is therefore highly likely that
young Walter had witnessed part of the construction of Bazalgette's
London sewerage network.

Harper Twelvetrees, as well as being a businessman of considerable
vision, drive and opportunity would also appear to have had a
caring side. In setting up his factory to manufacture laundry and
other products, which were sold in large quantities throughout the
old British Empire, he seems to have genuinely wanted to make
sure that ordinary working people had access to a range of cheap
commodities that would improve their personal hygiene and the
cleanliness of their homes. He had commented that he wished to
"encourage cleanliness among the poor by selling them a packet of
soap powder for a penny". This would equate to around 0.4 pence
today.

An article in *Shops and Companies of London*, edited by Henry Mayhew, published circa 1865, describes a visit to the Imperial Chemical Works by an unnamed chronicler. It allows an insight into the range of products manufactured by Harper Twelvetrees, who at the time was employing around 420 people. The reporter writes:

It is impossible to give the reader an adequate idea, other than by stating that there are no less than twelve distinct businesses comprised within one establishment, some of which are kept working night and day, and of which the following are the particulars:

1. A manufactory for the production of "Saponine" and Glycerine Soap Powders, as well as Washing Powders, which is said to be considerably larger than any similar establishment in the world.
2. A manufactory for Laundry Thumb and Blue Ball, Soluble Powder Blue and Liquid Blue.
3. A manufactory for Satin Enamel Starch, and Briggs' Australian Glaze Starch.
4. A manufactory for Blacking, in Paste and Liquid, and Harness Polishing Fluid.
5. A manufactory for Block Blacklead and Powder Lead.
6. A manufactory for Metallic Writing Inks and Marking Inks.
7. A manufactory for Baking and Pastry Powder, Yeastrine, and Egg and Butter Powders.
8. A small Soap Boiling plant for the production of Mottled and Pale Soaps, and a Re-melting plant for Perfumed Toilet Soaps.
9. A Chemical plant for the manufacture of Epsom Salts, and various Fine Chemicals.
10. An extensive grinding and packing business in Spices, Gingers, Rices, and various Miscellaneous Goods usually sold by Grocers in packets.
11. A wholesale business in Drysalters' Goods, Gums, Alum, Soda, Acids, Logwood, Saltpetre, Brimstone, Twines, Seeds, Etc., Etc.
12. A manufactory fitted with circular saws, lathes, and every requisite for the production of Clothes-Wringing Machines and other Washing Machinery.

To give an indication of the total number of products manufactured at the Imperial Chemical Works in a single year, it has been calculated that 101,843,464 labels were used for the identification of individual items. The success of Harper's business was probably due to the considerable amount of publicity he engaged in which, apart from the individual product labelling, had three strategic advertising strands. First the general public were made aware of the name Twelvetrees and his products by large letters painted on hoardings and walls, normally white lettering on a blue background to represent the colour of his powders and laundry blue. Second he would address the reading classes through advertisements in newspapers, magazines and journals and thirdly he would send what were classified as "illuminated show-bills" and trade catalogues to the shops that stocked his goods.

For the day, this degree of advertising was quite radical and occasionally it became the subject of criticism and derision by a few of Harper's non-progressive customers. To them, this form of promotion was nothing less than boasting. One amusing example of this can be seen in the correspondence (23 September 1864) of a Guildford shopkeeper who returned one of Harper's catalogues with the following remarks. "Sir, I beg to return the enclosed, as I seldom or ever have to do with puffing houses. Good articles will generally find their way with the public without such nonsense, to say the least of it. Remaining your obedient servant."

Harper Twelvetrees' Villa Washing and Wringing Machine manufactured at Bromley-by-Bow. It is described in Mary Isabella Beeton's book, *Beeton's Book of Household Management*, thus: "Harper Twelvetrees makes a specialty of the 'Villa Washing Machine' of which we give an illustration. Prices from 55s [£2.75p]. This is an excellent machine for family use, large enough for ordinary purposes, very easy to work, without being cumbersome, and, like all the machines manufactured by this firm, is very strong and durable."

Harper's measured response of around 800 words is a literary gem and a small part of it is reproduced here to give the reader a flavour of his reply.

> "Sir, I beg to acknowledge the receipt of your communication of the 23rd September (returning my wholesale catalogue), in which you inform me that you decline to do business with what you are pleased to characterise 'puffing houses'. I must beg of you to excuse me if I remark, that I had imagined that all the tradesmen of your antique stamp had died out long since, not having met with any such during the past twenty-five years that I have been engaged in commercial life."

History has shown that there is always a minority who will resist new ideas and not wish to embrace change, even if it can be demonstrated that there are future benefits to be had. Fortunately Harper Twelvetrees appears not to have been too hampered in this respect as an article by the editor of the *Stratford Times* (9

November 1861) shows. The editor begins the piece by first giving a description of Bromley-by-Bow in the following manner:

> It was the obscurest of obscure districts, and everything about the place tended to produce upon the mind an impression of stunted powers and dwarfish capabilities. Constituting, as it does, one of the fag-ends of the county of Middlesex, divided from the Essex marshes by the murky Lea (whose easy current forms, amongst other uses for which it is adapted, a main sewer which touches not the pockets of the ratepayers), there was some danger at one time of its being altogether overwhelmed by its more busy and flourishing neighbours, with whom communication was rendered difficult; for every outlet, street, or byway in the place appeared formed upon the most crooked, crazy, and circuitous principle imaginable. ….The smoke and stench arising from gas-factories, tan-works, glass-houses, bone grinders, etc., had blanched the face of vegetation and produced a striking anomaly in the market-gardens which once flourished in the neighbourhood.

A share certificate issued to a Mr Alec Wilson for two shares (£3 paid for each share) in Harper Twelvetrees Limited on 28 November 1865.

This rather damning and graphic description of the area continues, but I am sure that by now the reader will have got the picture.

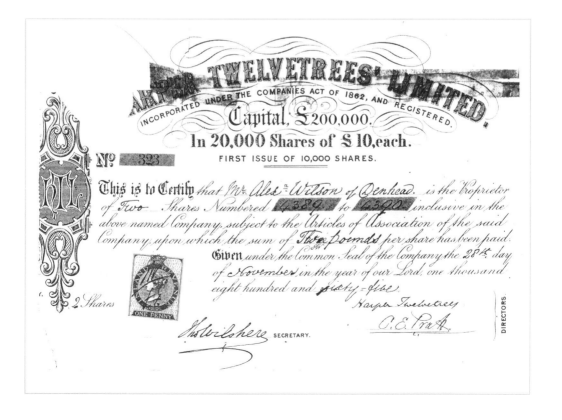

After depicting such a dismal scene and totally condemning the area, the editor's article becomes positively up-beat when he explains:

> But lately a great change has been apparent in the neighbourhood. Instead of dirty, narrow lanes bounded by high walls, now there are to be seen neat, commodious, and well-built cottages, flanking tidy roads. The old population is losing its distinctive traits before a new, fresh, and vigorous class that is rapidly settling amongst them, and giving an air of busy life and incessant occupation to a place, which once wore an empty gloom hardly redeemed by the wild rush of waters roaring in the adjacent mill-stream. ....One fact, however, must be borne in mind – one which becomes a matter of deep interest and moment, as affording some idea of what may be accomplished by the efforts of an unaided man. The change produced is attributed, to a very large extent, to the influence exercised by a single individual – and that individual is Mr. Harper Twelvetrees.

Harper Twelvetrees, unlike many factory owners of his generation, held the view that his workers would perform their duties better if he provided good working conditions and a number of fringe benefits. While it is always difficult to guess what motivates some bosses to provide decent working conditions for their employees, it is fairly clear that, for Harper Twelvetrees, there were more worthwhile goals in life other than just seeking profit.

Harper had a number of cottages built close to his factory to provide accommodation for his employees and their families. He also set up a lecture hall in a large workshop of a factory previously occupied by Messrs Hayter (as mentioned in Walter's correspondence, above) which was now part of his industrial complex. As an indication of Harper's commitment to the region, the wider community was allowed to use this facility for concerts and "select and popular entertainments". To improve the education of local people he provided the lecture hall with a well-stocked library and also arranged evening classes for adults. In 1862 a "sick and benevolent fund" was set up and all those joining the Imperial Chemical Works had to contribute one hour's pay each week. Members in need of relief were paid weekly in accordance with a graduated table based on the amount of contribution paid in. Once a year there was a meeting of the fund holders and any surplus that had accrued was paid back to the members in proportion to their contributions. The workers also enjoyed the facilities of a "clothing club" and a "penny savings bank" and on the leisure side the factory had its own brass band, a drum and fife band and a cricket club.

On Sundays the hall was used for religious worship and the preaching was said to be non-sectarian on account of "Christian ministers of all denominations having conducted the services". A Bible-class was held on Sunday afternoon "for the religious instruction of such young men as are disposed to seek it". No doubt considered politically correct at the time, "Mothers' Sewing Meetings" were held "for the improvement of the women in the locality".

On 4 November 1861, when the lecture hall officially opened, addresses were given by Acton S. Ayrton, M.P., the Sheriffs of London and Middlesex and John Cassell, the Rector of Bow. It was further reported that dignitaries came from all over the country to congratulate Harper Twelvetrees for his philanthropic contribution to the community. While more research is required to confirm, beyond doubt, the names of the prominent speakers who attended the regular meetings, held at what became known as the Institute, there is evidence to suggest that internationally famous people such as Robert Todd Lincoln (1843–1926) son of President Abraham Lincoln and the last United States Minister to Britain before the title changed to Ambassador, John Stuart Mill (1806–1873) British philosopher and economist, John Bright (1811–1889) British reformer and free trade advocate, and Lord Shaftesbury (Anthony Ashley Cooper, 1801–1885) social reformer and champion of Factory Acts and Mines Act, had all lectured there.

Bromley-by-Bow, a tiny east London district, was probably not the first place that would spring to mind as a platform for the great 19th-century reformers. However, it seems likely that Harper Twelvetrees, F.R.S.L., President of the Bromley Literary Association, member of the London Emancipation Committee and associated with a host of other important bodies, would have attracted the great and the good to the area, particularly when taking into account his high-profile, philanthropic image and his flair for advertising. The need to promote the Institute and to communicate to the outside world the benefits of working at the Imperial Chemical Works had not been overlooked either. This was done through the *Bromley Lecture-hall Chronicle*, a publication that journalists often used to supplement their articles.

In 1865, after only seven years in business at Three Mills Lane, with all the attendant fanfare and publicity surrounding the product range, Harper Twelvetrees put his Imperial Chemical Works up for sale. The business and premises were sold to a limited company for £53,852-8s-5d and in the following year the General Trading Company Limited purchased the business. At some point during these proceedings, Harper appears to have moved to Dublin. According to the reported Court records, under Adjourned Sittings for Examination and Discharge, 24 November 1868, the General Trading Company Limited was in the process of liquidation and, as a consequence, Harper Twelvetrees had been declared bankrupt. He had only been paid £791-5s of the agreed purchase money for the Imperial Chemical Works.

When granting the order of discharge, the Judge observed that:

> the Bankrupt was entitled to great sympathy on account of his severe losses, and that it must always be a matter of great regret to find a person who, from a position of affluence, had fallen through his connection with Public Companies. The Bankrupt had assisted his Assignees to the extent of his ability, and had given his evidence very satisfactory, and the order of discharge would be granted.

No doubt many in this position would have called it a day; not so Harper Twelvetrees who was about to show the world the meaning of the words morality and determination.

We pick up the threads of the story once more from a "special price list for export and wholesale merchants", published by the newly formed business of Harper Twelvetrees and Son, Cordova Works, Grove Road, Bow, London, and begin to piece together the jigsaw. Interestingly, a paragraph has been included at the foot of the price list entitled, "An Explanation". The paragraph is in the form of a communication to Harper's present and former customers, setting out the reasons why he became bankrupt. When reading his account and noting that Harper had apparently the confidence to go into print about the unfortunate episode of his demise, this might indicate that the liquidators had treated him shabbily. In the text Harper explained to his customers that:

> not having been paid by the Company for [his] Business, (except £791-5s on account of the purchase) [he] then offered to take back his Property, and release all claims on the Company. That offer was, however, refused by the Liquidators, who transferred to one of their personal Friends the valuable property which Harper Twelvetrees had accumulated by unremitting toil and anxiety of several years, and for which only the above nominal sum had been paid to him by the Company – thus leaving Harper Twelvetrees at liberty to re-establish himself in Business in his own name, without infringing the rights of any individual whatever.

While Harper's financial state would have been a strong and motivating influence to tempt him back into business, from what we have so far learned of the man it would be difficult to imagine that personal gain was the sole reason for his decision to return. An evening meeting arranged by Harper's professional acquaintances and friends, and held at Radley's Hotel, Blackfriars, to celebrate his return to business, supports this notion. During the evening's proceedings "numerous congratulatory letters from various wholesale City firms, provincial merchants and absent friends were read" and the chairman referred to Harper's "laborious efforts on behalf of the moral, social, intellectual and religious welfare of the

SPECIAL PRICE LIST FOR EXPORT & WHOLESALE MERCHANTS.

HARPER TWELVETREES AND SON,
Cordova Works, Grove Road, Bow, London, E.
SOLE MANUFACTURERS OF HARPER TWELVETREES' ORIGINAL PATENT

GLYCERINE SOAP POWDER,
CLEANSING CRYSTALS AND OTHER WASHING POWDERS, BALL BLUE, BLACK LEAD, BAKING POWDER, &c., &c.

Respectfully inform their WHOLESALE and EXPORT CUSTOMERS, that having considerably enlarged their MANUFACTURING PREMISES, they now possess unequalled facilities for the execution of Orders, for a continuance of which they will feel greatly honoured and obliged.

☞ HARPER TWELVETREES & SON'S Export Glycerine Soap Powder is SPECIALLY PREPARED for the climates of Australia, New Zealand, United States, Canada, South Africa, the Mediterranean Ports, and the West Indies. Every Packet guaranteed to be of the same quality as formerly manufactured by HARPER TWELVETREES, the INVENTOR, PATENTEE, and ORIGINAL MANUFACTURER, and to contain FOUR TIMES THE WASHING STRENGTH OF ANY OTHER WASHING POWDER.

HARPER TWELVETREES & SON'S WASHING & SOAP POWDERS.

	Per Gross.
GLYCERINE SOAP POWDER FOR EXPORT } Specially prepared and guaranteed	5/-
LAUNDRY SOAP POWDER, Penny Packets 4oz.	5/6
No. 1 DRY SOAP—Kiln-dried Tallow Soap, 2oz.	5/-
GLYCERISED SOAP POWDER, 2oz.	5/-
ORIGINAL SOAP POWDER, 2oz.	4/-
WASHING & CLEANSING CRYSTALS, 2oz.	3/6
ORIGINAL WASHING POWDER, (not Soap Powder) 2oz.	3/6
ECONOMICAL SOAP POWDER, 6oz. very large	7/-

DRY SOAP, in 4oz. & 8oz. Tinfoil Packets, 28/- per cwt.

HARPER TWELVETREES & SON'S Pure & Genuine Baking Powders.
First Manufactured by HARPER TWELVETREES in 1848.

No. 1, Best Baking and Pastry Powder, in Bottles for EXPORTATION, various sizes.

Shilling Canisters	6/6 per doz.
Sixpenny	3/9 "
Penny Packets	6/- per gross.

No. 2, Superior Baking Powder:—

Penny Packets	5/- per gross.
Sixpenny Canisters	3/6 per doz.
Shilling	6/- "

No. 3, Economical Baking Powder:—

Penny Packets	4/- per gross.
Smaller Packets	2/9 "

RICE STARCH.

In 5lb. papers, Best Quality	30/- per cwt.
In 4oz., 8oz., and 16oz., packets	34/- "
In 2oz.	36/- "
No. 1 LONDON RICE STARCH in papers,	28/- "
DOUBLE REFINED POWDER STARCH, green label, 2oz., 4oz., 8oz., and 16oz.	
7lb. packets	32/- "

HARPER TWELVETREES & SON'S LAUNDRY BALL BLUE.
Is unequalled in any market for Quality at the price. COMPARE SAMPLES.

In 1oz. and 4oz. Balls, 4 and 7lb. boxes	40/- per cwt.
Very Brilliant Quality	46/- "
If ½oz. & ½ Balls 2/- extra. If 1lb. and 2lb. boxes 2/6 more.	
FAMILY Sixpenny boxes	45/- per gross.

INDIGO THUMB & LION BLUE.
In ¼oz. ½oz. and 1oz. Thumbs or Cakes, at 7d., 8d., 9d.,

BLACK LEADS IN POWDER.
PURE PENCIL LEAD, Æ Quality the finest imported, 1oz., 2oz., 4oz.,

and 8oz. packets	40/- per cwt.

Packed in TINFOIL for Exportation.

No. 1, Pencil Lead in green label	30/- "
" 2, " superior	24/- "
" 3, " Red Labels	18/- "
" 4, Servants' Friend, White Labels	15/- "

Customers' name and address on Labels for 1cwt. each size.

BLOCK BLACK LEAD.

NICKEL SILVER (Registered) BLACK LEAD, in 1oz., 2oz., and 4oz. blocks	5/- per box.
PURE PENCIL LEAD, Æ quality	40/- per cwt.
No. 1, Ditto	30/- "
" 2, Ditto superior	24/- "
" 3, Ditto in 7lb. papers	18/- "
BALL BLACK LEAD	24/- "

SCENTED HAIR OIL, RED OR PALE.

Sixpenny Bottles	4/- per dozen.
Shilling ditto	7/- "
Large ditto 10/- 12/- and 14/-	"
Loose, in Casks or Tins	5/6 per gallon.

WRITING INKS.
BLACK, Penny Glass Bottles, various shapes, capsuled,

	5/- per gross.
" " sealed	4/6 "
" SIX-PENNY stone bottles	2/9 per doz.
" SHILLING " Pint bottles 5/6	
BLUE, Penny Glass Bottles	5/- per gross.

MISCELLANEOUS.

EPSOM SALTS, 1oz. packets, 7lb. boxes, per cwt.	
Loose in casks	"
CARBONATE OF SODA, 1oz. packets, 7lb. boxes	"
Loose in casks	"
CARBONATE OF MAGNESIA, 1d. packets 7/- per gross	
CREAM OF TARTAR, 1oz., and in packets	
SENNA LEAVES, ½d. packets, 3/6 per gross, and	
penny packets, 6/- per gross.	
FLOUR OF SULPHUR, 1oz., 2oz., 4oz. 24/- per cwt	
MILK OF SULPHUR, 1d. packets, 7lb. boxes	
VENETIAN RED, 2oz., and 4oz. 14/- "	
ROTTEN STONE, best 2oz., and 4oz. 14/- "	
TARTARIC ACID, (English make) powdered in casks.	
GUM ARABIC, Loose, 9d. per pound and upwards.	
NURSERY VOILET POWDER, penny packets and	
quarter gross boxes, 5/- per gross.	
PREPARED FULLERS EARTH, penny packets, and	
quarter gross boxes. 5/- per gross.	

Part of a price list issued by Harper Twelvetrees when starting the new business of Harper Twelvetrees and Son after his discharge as a bankrupt. Note that the address is now Cordova Works, Grove Road, Bow, London, East.

working classes". Having the support of so many former customers, business and community acquaintances might indicate that Harper was in the process of making good any outstanding debts that had accrued from the sale of his former business. Being discharged from bankruptcy would have meant that all Harper's debts would have been written off. We may never know the real reason why Harper returned to resurrect his former business and we can only speculate on the likely reasons. For example, he may have wished to make a moral contribution by making good any losses his suppliers might have suffered when he did not receive the agreed amount for his business (it is possible that he was relying on the sale of his business to clear invoices for material received etc.). On the other hand it could have been more a case of wishing to see his once-prosperous company back on its feet and trading again. Whatever the reasons, apart from trying to make good his personal losses as a discharged bankrupt, there was no legal requirement to take the action he did.

Harper Twelvetrees' Will, made on 9 October 1881, tells us that he was living at 223 Evering Road, Upper Clapton, Middlesex (now in the London borough of Hackney). A second address, 80 Finsbury Pavement, in the City of London (recorded in the Will) would suggest that this was a business address, probably the Company office. From the letterhead of a 1932 communication, it was revealed that a company bearing the name Harper Twelvetrees Ltd., Makers of the "Villa" Washing and Mangling Machines was in operation at 24 City Road, Finsbury Square, London, EC1, but it would appear that his son Walter Noble was not involved in the business.

Harper Twelvetrees died prematurely in November 1881 at the age of 58, only a month after writing his Will. His early death deprived us of learning more about the man. Had he lived to a reasonable age, one might speculate that we may have seen an autobiography from a man who, after all, was the President of the Bromley Literary Association. However, this early research into Harper Twelvetrees' life has alerted readers in the 21st century to the unfinished story of this truly remarkable man. Having set up his business in London's lower Lea Valley, we have seen that, through a combination of philanthropy and humanity, Harper Twelvetrees was able to change radically the social and economic conditions that existed in the impoverished area of 19th-century Bromley-by-Bow. From such beginnings one would have expected the area to have gone from strength to strength. Sadly, little remains today as a memorial to Harper's humanity.

The Tesco store at Bromley-by-Bow that now, along with its southern car park, occupies the site of the former Harper Twelvetrees Imperial Chemical Works. In the background and to the left of the picture can be seen the Clock Mill at Three Mills.

REFERENCES

Author unknown, Article from *Stratford Times*, 9 November, 1861.

Lewis, Jim, *London's Lea Valley, Britain's Best Kept Secret*, Phillimore & Co. Ltd., Chichester, 1999.

Mayhew, Henry (ed.), *Shops and Companies of London*, Richard Barrett, London.

Mew, Elizabeth, the great, great granddaughter of Harper Twelvetrees, (a personal conversation, February 2000, and the loan of family material).

Tower Hamlets Local History Library, Tower Hamlets, London (file containing correspondence and newspaper cuttings on Harper Twelvetrees and the Imperial Chemical Works).

APPENDIX 1

JOHN ANDERSON THE RUNAWAY SLAVE

The author wrote the story of the 19th-century entrepreneur, industrialist and philanthropist, Harper Twelvetrees in his book, *London's Lea Valley More Secrets Revealed*, published in 2001. At the time it was not fully appreciated that Harper Twelvetrees was deeply involved in helping to promote the plight of a runaway American slave, Jack Burton and, through The British and Foreign Anti-Slavery Society, brought Burton to England.

Jack Burton (born about 1830) was the slave of a plantation owner, Moses Burton of Fayette, Missouri. Not long after he was born, Jack's father managed to escape from his owner. Later, when Jack was about seven, his mother was sold to a slave trader and the lad effectively became an orphan. Young Jack was befriended by the plantation owner's wife and while growing up he appears to have become proficient in most of the jobs around the estate.

John Anderson, formerly Jack Burton, a runaway American slave who came to England in 1861 and was supported by Harper Twelvetrees.

In December 1850 Jack married Marie Tomlin, a slave who lived close to the Burton estate. She had two children from a previous marriage and in their short time together Marie and Jack were to have a child of their own. Less than three years after their marriage, in August 1853, Jack was sold for $1,000 to a farmer in Slaine County, Missouri. Slaves, under the law, were the property of their masters and his owner forbade Jack to see his wife and child. However, Jack nurtured ideas of escape to Canada, at the time part of the British Empire, but before doing so he illegally visited his wife to tell her of his plan.

While escaping Jack, now with a reward on his head for capture, was pursued and eventually apprehended by a local farmer Seneca Diggs, and in the ensuing struggle Diggs was killed. In about September 1853, with the help of abolitionists, Jack finally made it to Canada. There he settled in Windsor and eventually got work as a plasterer and a labourer. To escape identification as a fugitive, he adopted the name of John Anderson.

In 1854 the American government requested Anderson's extradition, but Lord Elgin, the Governor General of British North America, would not issue the warrant. However, in April 1860, a local magistrate jailed Anderson on a charge of murder but his release was secured by a Hamilton attorney, Samuel Freeman. Anderson was sent to prison again in October 1860 on a warrant issued by a three-magistrate court after it had received sworn affidavits from persons in Missouri. The charge was again murder. Supported by local abolitionists, Anderson's lawyers, in January 1861, obtained a writ of *habeas corpus* from the Court of Queens Bench in London. In Canada this action was looked upon as an act of interference. However, before the writ could be served in Canada, Anderson's lawyers had appealed to the Court of Common Pleas in Toronto and Chief Justice William Draper, on 16 February 1861, discharged Anderson on what was essentially a technicality, in that the warrant from the magistrate's court had not actually accused Anderson of murder. The whole episode became a major issue in British–American relations.

Anderson was invited to England by The British and Foreign Anti-Slavery Society and arrived in the country about June 1861. A celebratory meeting welcoming Anderson to England, chaired by Harper Twelvetrees, was held at Exeter Hall, London. The meeting was attended by many prominent people including Members of Parliament, leading Quakers and clergy of different denominations and several made speeches from the platform in praise of Anderson.

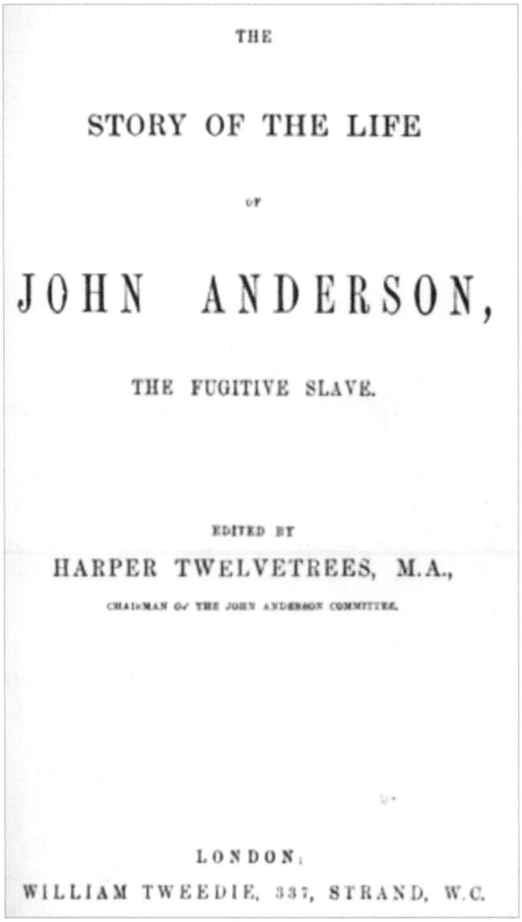

THE

STORY OF THE LIFE

OF

JOHN ANDERSON,

THE FUGITIVE SLAVE.

EDITED BY

HARPER TWELVETREES, M.A.,

CHAIRMAN OF THE JOHN ANDERSON COMMITTEE.

LONDON:
WILLIAM TWEEDIE, 337, STRAND, W.C.

The book on the life and plight of John Anderson the fugitive American slave, edited by Harper Twelvetrees.

Between July and September 1861, John Anderson fulfilled invitations to speak at about 25 meetings, mainly in London and southern England. In December 1861 he enrolled at the British Training Institution at Corby, Northamptonshire where he remained for one year. On 24 December, 1861 he set sail for the Republic of Liberia and, to date, nothing appears to be known of his fate. Fortunately, while in England, he must have been interviewed at some length by Harper Twelvetrees as in 1863 a book was published, edited by Harper, *The Story of the Life of John Anderson, the Fugitive Slave*.

REFERENCES

Reinders, Robert, *Dictionary of Canadian Biography Online*, University of Toronto, 2000.

Twelvetrees, Harper, *The Story of the Life of John Anderson, the Fugitive Slave*, William Tweedie, London, 1863.

8. FLOUR POWER IN THE LEA VALLEY

In 1867 George Reynolds Wright came to Enfield and entered into partnership with James Dilly Young, the miller of Ponders End Mill, taking up residence in the East Mill House. The house, built in the reign of Queen Anne, is in active use today providing the necessary accommodation to administer the only independent, family-run flour mill in London. Speaking to directors and staff of this company will immediately reveal a love and enthusiasm for a proud tradition of milling at Ponders End, whose roots can be traced back as far as Domesday.

By the early years of the 17th century the mill was known as Flanders Mill. Power to drive the seven pairs of millstones came from the River Lea via two breast water wheels. Evidence of this earlier water power can still be observed today. If a visitor stands on the bridge, which is part of the Lea Valley Road running between the King George and William Girling reservoirs, and looks north, a weir will be seen which allows water from the river to enter the mill head stream that passes directly below them. In the 18th century the mill became known as Enfield Mill, changing its name again halfway through the 19th century to Ponders End Mill.

George Reynolds Wright (1824–1914) founder of Wright's Mill at Ponders End.

In the early days of milling, flour had to be delivered to the bakeries of London and the surrounding area by horse-drawn wagon. A typical day for the carman would start around 6am when he would leave the mill with a full load of five tons, ensuring the route he took did not have too many steep and difficult slopes. After a round trip of some 10 to 20 miles he would return at about 7pm, not finishing the day until his main asset, the horses, had been fed, watered and stabled. Next day, an appointed operative would come to work early in the morning to see that the horses were harnessed and ready for the day's deliveries.

By 1909 the new technology of electricity had become the energy source and traditional methods of powering the mill, water and steam, were abandoned. This also gave the opportunity to replace the ageing millstones, which required regular maintenance and dressing by skilled craftsmen, with modern efficient roller machinery which, at the time, was being introduced almost universally by the milling industry. However, some of the millstones were retained up until the 1960s by Wright's, who were committed to maintaining a service to a number of their customers who required specialist flour.

Oldest known picture of Wright's Mill c.1880.

The early 20th century also brought with it an improved road network and in August 1906 the Company took advantage of this by acquiring a steam wagon. This new technology dramatically increased the amount of flour which could be transported compared to the horse-drawn wagon. However, steam wagons of the day had certain drawbacks. Initially these vehicles had solid iron wheels which caused considerable problems for their drivers when descending or ascending hills with bulk loads of between 15 and 20 tons, particularly when the roads were icy or wet.

Those were hard times for our ancestors but we can be proud of their achievements, which have helped successive generations of

Women workers on the pre-pack line at Wright's Mill c.1948.

Wright's Mill delivery fleet c.1950.

Wrights to invest confidently in the future of the mill, preserving part of the Lea Valley's rich industrial heritage.

The year 1938 brought a significant leap forward in the fortunes of the mill when the directors, no doubt with expansion firmly in mind, purchased, from the Metropolitan Water Board, freehold ownership of a little over 11 acres of surrounding land and the entitlement of passage for barges from and to the Lee Navigation.

When the Second World War commenced in 1939 the mill came under government control. To help secure food supplies for the nation and to supplement the losses caused by the bombing of the mills situated in the London Docks, the production at Ponders End was considerably increased. This was achieved by extending the working of the mill to seven days a week and 52 weeks a year for the duration of the war. Fortunately the mill did not suffer any serious damage from enemy action, although the constant operation of the plant had taken its toll on the machinery.

By the early 1950s, with the mill back in family control, the decision was taken to modernise and refurbish the plant and machinery. The specialist firm of Thomas Robinson of Rochdale was called in and by April that year, only ten weeks after modernisation began, the mill recommenced production with a 50 per cent increase in capacity. Flour could now be processed at the rate of twelve 280lb sacks per hour.

Company expansion still continues beyond the millennium with improvements in buildings and equipment and the introduction of silos for bulk storage of grain and flour. Modern methods of production call for changes to the way in which flour is

Wheat arriving at Wright's Mill by barge on the River Lea c.1955.

transported, so Wright's have invested in bulk road tankers. No doubt the 19th-century wagon driver would have found these new methods of storage and delivery impossible to imagine.

Not resting on their laurels, the directors of Wright's have responded to changing public tastes by introducing a number of new product lines, particularly aimed at today's busy consumer. Speciality flours and bread mixes, which can be made quickly and easily, now appear on several supermarket shelves and expansion into overseas markets is an ongoing feature of the business strategy. With an eye on changing consumer eating habits, and never wishing to miss an opportunity, the directors, some years ago,

One of Wright's covered delivery lorries outside the old mill building c.1954.

decided to produce speciality flours for the growing number of pizza and poppadom manufacturers.

Over the years many Lea Valley companies have come and gone, but Wright's Mill stands as a glowing example of determination and entrepreneurship, a symbol of the ability of a family business to adapt product and processes to the needs of a highly competitive and ever-changing industrial world.

The example of progression from Wright's early Lea Valley roots and the company's successful expansion into the 21st century must surely act, not only as encouragement to other firms wishing to set up in the region, but as a continuing reminder of how to adapt and prosper. Here are important lessons for us all to learn and perhaps the Wright's model can supply some valuable clues for industry in general, pointing the way to future regeneration of the region.

APPENDIX 2

REACHING FOR THE FUTURE

The author, in his former industrial role, has worked with businesses within eastern and western Europe and from the Middle East to the Far East and has never come across an operation quite like Wright's Mill. The mill has successfully incorporated a range of buildings, some listed, and some which date from the 16th century, into an efficient modern-day manufacturing facility.

Anyone visiting Wright's Mill in the late 20th century could not fail to become immersed in an atmosphere of energy and also be impressed by the forward thinking of the management as the company looked for new and challenging business opportunities. This 'can do' spirit led to the decision to greatly expand and modernise the production facilities, a step not taken lightly as there were considerable long-term cost implications. Once the decision was taken, things moved quickly. In 2000, new warehouses were built and Buhler's, the Swiss Milling Engineers, were commissioned to install state-of-the-art high-speed packaging and palletising equipment. When the then English Cricket Captain, Nasser Hussain, opened the newly built units in November 2001, they were acclaimed as the most sophisticated packaging and storage facilities in Europe.

The Ponders End site now consists of a blend of ancient and modern buildings. However, the casual visitor could be forgiven for

New buildings at Wright's Mill, Ponders End.

thinking that the facilities and processes behind some of the more elderly facades matched their quaint exteriors, but these assumptions would be totally wrong. For example, once inside the old mill itself it is perfectly possible to imagine that you have somehow been transported into another dimension. Inside is a multitude of sparkling modern milling machinery that allows the mill to comply with the exacting regulatory standards and procedures of ISO 9000 and also the stringent Hazard Analysis Critical Control Points (HACCPs).

Investment in an on-site laboratory and bakery has allowed sampling and testing to be carried out at each stage of production and every delivery of wheat arriving at the mill is also sampled by an automatic probe and the results recorded. Not satisfied with the high level of quality control that that has been put in place, Wright's management wished to investigate the environmental impact of their manufacturing processes. To this end they commissioned an independent audit of their operations and the resulting recommendations have been implemented.

It is clear that the heavy investment in plant and machinery and also the detailed attention to product quality is already paying off

16kg bags being filled with pizza flour.

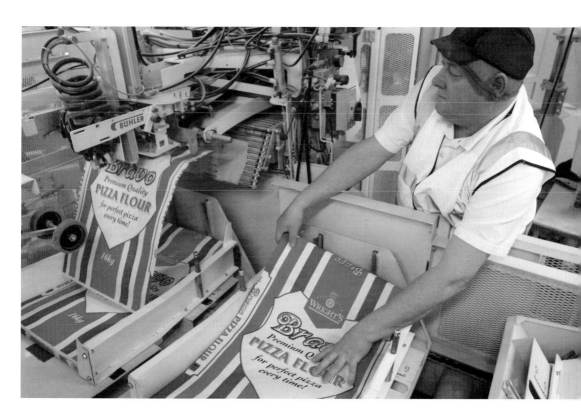

as export opportunities have opened up to the West Indies, France, Bulgaria and Belgium. This resulted in recognition for the company when the Managing Director, David Wright received the prestigious crystal trophy presented by the organisers of the Trade and Investments Passport to Export programme. This was followed, in 2004, when Wright's Flour won the Manufacturer of the Year at the London Business Awards.

A pallet containing 32kg bags ready to be wrapped.

Many companies might feel that once they had invested considerable sums in new plant and machinery they could relax for a time, but not Wright's, as the programme of investment and the developing of new products continues apace. David Wright is the fifth generation of the family involved with milling at Ponders End since his ancestor entered the business in the 1860s and still has the enthusiasm for developing the business further. Fortunately there is a sixth generation of the Wright family maturing in the wings.

An operator working on a modern packing line.

Flour discharge heads above a filling station.

Some of the sophisticated Buhler process machinery that controls the daily work of Wright's Mill.

REFERENCES

Interviews with David Wright, the current Chairman and Managing Director of G.R. Wright & Sons Ltd. and also members of staff.

Wright, G.R. & Sons Ltd., *The Story of a Family Business*, undated brochure.

Note

Wright's Mill is the only family-owned flour mill operating in the Greater London area.

9. FROM BARROW BOY TO FOOD TYCOON – A LEGEND IN HIS LIFETIME

Jacob Cohen was born in Whitechapel in London's East End, into a poor emigrant family from Poland, on 29 October 1898. His father, Avroam, a harsh disciplinarian by all accounts, had lived with his wife and family in abject poverty while working as a tailor in the sweatshops of London. By long hours and sacrifice he was able to move his family to 26 Darnley Road, Hackney where he established himself as a jobbing tailor, doing sub-contract work for manufacturers in the garment trade.

Young Jacob, who had begun school at the age of six, left education when he was only 14 and like many children of his generation he had school reports which carried the not untypical remarks, "must try harder" and "lacks application". With the young man's career prospects looking decidedly bleak, he first began work for his brother-in-law, Morris Israel, in the street markets of London. After a short spell in the market he joined his father's tailoring business and worked long hours into the night making buttonholes in jackets, for which he received only pocket money. Jacob hated the long hours and the strict regime of his father's business and looked for an opportunity to escape.

Sir John (Jack) Cohen (1898–1979).

In March 1917, at the age of 18, he enlisted in the Royal Flying Corps (RFC) as an air mechanic. After completing his basic training, during which he suffered racial abuse, he reluctantly allowed himself to be known as Jack rather than Jacob to avoid making his ethnic origins obvious. His first posting was to Roehampton where he worked as a rigger on barrage balloons before being sent to the Middle East. While entering Alexandria harbour his troopship was torpedoed by an enemy submarine and Jack, a non-swimmer, was almost drowned. Luckily he survived this ordeal and the rest of his war was relatively uneventful. He was demobilised from the RFC in 1919.

Jack's reward for war service, along with many of his contemporaries, was unemployment, a fate that certainly did not suit his character. Although his father had asked him on a number of occasions to join his tailoring business, Jack did not relish the thought of losing his hard-won independence. With limited skills to offer, Jack's mind drifted back to the time when he had worked for his brother-in-law in the street markets. Now, with a demobilisation gratuity of £30, Jack hired a barrow and invested the rest in a quantity of ex-NAAFI (Navy, Army and Air Force Institutes) foodstuffs. Pushing his barrow to Well Street, Hackney, in London's East End, Jack was fortunate in being able to rent part of a site from a market trader. In his first day of trading he sold £4's worth of groceries, of which 25 per cent was profit. Soon Jack mastered the "show business" ways of the market traders, selling tinned milk, not at threepence, not at twopence – "it's yours for a penny". Broken biscuits, golden syrup, tinned jam etc., were all disposed of in a similar way to his working-class customers who were always on the lookout for a bargain. In the harsh reality of East End life, low prices were a key to Jack's growing success. Within six months of starting his business, Jack was trading in at least two other East End markets. It would appear that Jack had found his real niche in life and, as his biographer has pointed out, he had become not only a tradesman but also an entertainer.

The next few years were quite eventful for Jack. He moved his stock out of his father's house, which had virtually become a warehouse, and took a small lock-up in Clarence Road, Clapton, east London to store his ever-increasing amount of goods, until larger premises were found in the Upper Clapton Road. By 1920 an account was opened with the Midland Bank in Hackney, a sensible move as the takings from one of his stalls in the Caledonian Market had

Well Street market, Hackney, where Jack Cohen began his early career in groceries.

exceeded £100 in a single day. In only two years Jack was operating from around six London markets and he had also established himself as a supplier of groceries to other traders. In January 1924 Jack married Sarah (Cissie) Fox and her £500 dowry, along with £130 in wedding gifts, was wisely placed in a Post Office savings account. A house was rented in Gore Road, Hackney and it was there that their two children were born, Irene in 1926 and Shirley in 1930.

In late 1924, although he did not realise it at the time, Jack Cohen was about to take on new business that would prove to be a lasting tribute to his entrepreneurial skills. During his buying and selling

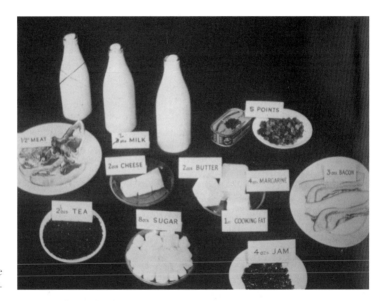

One person's weekly wartime food ration.

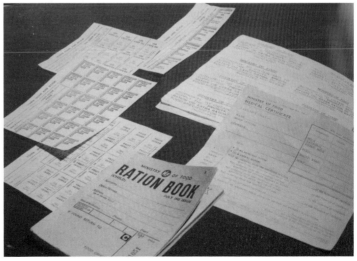

Wartime ration book and coupons that ensured each person received a fair share of available food from the retailer.

Goods being off-loaded at the first Tesco self-service store at St Albans, Hertfordshire, c1950.

Pile them high and sell them cheap. A typical Tesco store in the 1950s after World War Two food rationing ended.

forays in the food trade Jack had met T.E. Stockwell, a partner in the tea-importing business of Torring and Stockwell. Jack arranged to buy tea from the company in bulk at ninepence (3.7p) a pound and to sell it on in half-pound packs at sixpence (2.5p) each, a mark-up of 25 per cent. A brand name for the tea was established by combining the initials of his supplier, T.E. Stockwell, with the first two letters of Cohen making the now famous name of the food giant TESCO.

Jack Cohen died in 1979 after creating a retail empire that would change the shopping habits of the buying public forever. The name

A typical 1970s Tesco supermarket.

Tesco lives on as a fitting epitaph to this entrepreneurial man, not just in Britain but internationally. However, it is doubtful that the majority of customers flocking daily through the doors of the company's supermarkets around the world could remotely guess how the name Tesco came about.

Diana, the Princess of Wales, shopping at Tesco, Southport c.1990.

REFERENCES

Archer, Fiona, Interview at Tesco Head Office, February 2000.

Powell, David, *Counter Revolution, the Tesco Story*, Grafton Books, London, 1991.

10. EAST LONDON'S HOLLYWOOD

The 1890s saw the emergence of the film industry as early experiments took place with movie cameras in both Europe and America. By 1896, the Lumière Brothers had given the first public showing of moving pictures in Britain at the Regent Street Polytechnic (now the University of Westminster). Travelling showmen picked up the ideas of these early pioneers and began to whet the public appetite for the new entertainment by making films and showing them at fairgrounds and in village halls. In this way the British film industry was born.

As the 20th century flickered into life, Walthamstow, in east London, emerged as one of the first centres of the British film industry. In 1896, E.G. Turner appears to have been one of the earliest local pioneers when he gave the first film show at the Victoria Hall, the site of the former Granada cinema in Hoe Street, Walthamstow. He continued to show films locally, on Saturday afternoons, at the public baths in Walthamstow High Street, which once stood close to the northern end of Selborne Walk. Turner seems to have been an extraordinary man, giving up a career as a hairdresser to become an inventor, filmmaker and exhibitor. As early as 1904, his company (The Walthamstow Co.), later to become Walturdaw in 1905, was probably the first to create a film rental market in Britain. Turner publicly claimed that he had invented, and shown, the first talkie. He did this by synchronising a gramophone to a film projector and called his system the Cinematophone.

Precision was the first purpose-built film studio to appear in Walthamstow (1910) and the first in Britain with a glass-covered daylight stage. The studio was located at 280 Wood Street, on the west side near Whipps Cross, where modern flats now stand. A former roller-skating rink near the junction of Grove Road and Hoe Street appears to have been the next Walthamstow film studio when the British and Colonial Kinematograph Company relocated from East Finchley in October 1913. The company specialised in making travel films and had completed projects in Jamaica and Italy. In 1914, a disused horse tram shed at 588, Lea Bridge Road, Bakers

Arms, Leyton was to become the next film studio, being occupied by the I.B. Davison Film Company. The building was converted into a modern "dark stage" studio, with the principal area being illuminated by 35 arc lamps. Facilities were also installed to allow the studio the luxury of processing film on site.

The fourth studio, which was purpose built, in October 1914, at 245 Wood Street, Walthamstow (near Buck Walk) was that of Cunard Films Limited. Previously, the site had been occupied by Elm Cottage, which was demolished to make way for the new development. For its day the studio was technically state of the art, with a glass-roofed stage that could be illuminated further by 30 arc lamps and a searchlight. Workshop space, film processing laboratories and prop stores were all accommodated on site along with a small theatre for showing rushes. In 1915, Wallet Waller, one of the Cunard founders, died and the studio closed. Soon afterwards, in the summer of 1916, the site was taken over by the Broadwest film company, owned by G.T. Broadbridge and the producer Walter West. The studio quickly built up a team of leading actors and became the best known of the Walthamstow film companies.

A rare archive picture of a man using a J.A. Prestwich (J.A.P.) motion picture camera said to be c.1900. On the back of the photograph it is recorded that the man is G.T. West. It is possible that these initials are incorrect and that the camera operator is the producer Walter West of Broadwest Studio fame. Later poor quality photographs of Walter West show him without moustache.

Walthamstow had been chosen as a suitable location by many film companies as it was relatively close to London's West End and this allowed the actors, who had been "borrowed" from the theatre, to return on the well-connected railway to their stage roles after a day of filming. It was also thought that the air was clearer for outside filming in the outer London boroughs and it was further thought that there was less likelihood of the area suffering from the debilitating fogs that frequently brought the capital to a standstill. There were other good reasons for choosing Walthamstow - plenty of readymade film locations. Epping Forest could be a substitute for a whole range of movie backdrops from cowboy films to historic battle scenes. The former Cooperative Society's cobbled yard in Wood Street often doubled for scenes of yesteryear and the front aspect of the Clock House (Wood Street) could become an imposing mansion or a stately home.

Filming *The Life of Shakespeare* at the studio of the British and Colonial Kinematograph Company in Hoe Street, Walthamstow (c.1916).

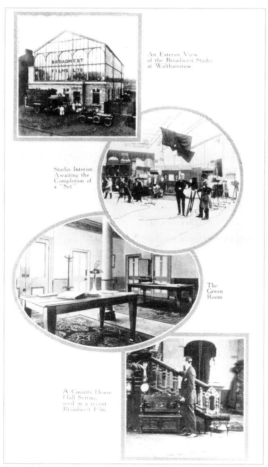

Broadwest Studio in Wood Street, Walthamstow (c.1916–1924).

The mid-1920s was an exceptionally bad time for the British film industry with many companies going out of business. Broadwest, the last of the Walthamstow studios, was sold in August 1926 to George Banfield and Leslie Eveleigh, the founders of British Filmcraft. This company was specifically set up to take advantage of the opportunities created by the Cinematograph Films Act. This new legislation required distributors and exhibitors to take a fixed quota of British films and this, in turn, spawned the production of what became known as "quota quickies". By the early 1930s, British Filmcraft had changed its name to Audible Filmcraft and in 1932 the company ceased trading, bringing the filmmaking era in Walthamstow to an end. However, these film studios were not the area's only connection with filmmaking.

An early picture of the Islington Film Studios, once a power station, where Alfred Hitchcock made some of his early films.

On 13 August 1899, in a room above his father's greengrocers shop at 517 High Road, Leytonstone, east London, Alfred Joseph Hitchcock was born. The boy, who would grow up to be a famous film director and also to be dubbed 'the Master of Suspense', spent his early childhood only a short distance away from the centre of the Walthamstow movie industry. Could the closeness have been an influencing factor in the choice of Hitchcock's later profession? This is a question that may never be answered, as little is known of the early life of this rather private man. No evidence exists which allows us to connect Hitchcock to the Walthamstow film industry which, by the time he had established his film career, had all but disappeared. Hitchcock's work was done elsewhere.

The Gainsborough Studios were set up as the Islington Studios at the junction of Poole Street and New North Road in 1919, on the Hackney side of the Grand Union Canal. Calling the building the Islington Studios has, for many years, proved irksome to many Hackney historians. It was the American Players-Lasky Film Company that first decided to make the run-down carpet warehouse by the canal (formerly a power station) their British base. By mid-1920 the building had been rapidly converted into a

A picture of the
Gainsborough Studio
(formerly Islington Film
Studios) taken in 1999 before
the building was redeveloped
as apartments.

modern state-of-the-art studio with three film stages, a large sunken
tank with windows for filming sea scenes and a comprehensive
range of workshops for scenery and other activities. However, the
handful of films produced by the Americans was judged
unsuccessful and in 1922 the decision was taken to hire the studios
out to other filmmakers. Cutting their losses, Players-Lasky pulled
out in 1924, presenting producers Michael Balcon and Mike Cutts,
who had made several successful films there, with an opportunity
to purchase the business. They were successful in raising the
necessary finance and Gainsborough Pictures was born.

Hitchcock's early film career began as a title card designer at the
Islington Studios in 1921 and in the following year he was
appointed assistant director on the film *Woman to Woman*. In 1925
he got his big break when Michael Balcon invited him to direct *The
Pleasure Garden* (1926), a film shot mainly in Germany that rapidly

Alfred Hitchcock with James Stewart at the Universal City Studios.

became a success. Other successes followed and Hitchcock soon became established as a highly competent director. One of his better-known early films, *The Lady Vanishes*, was made at the Gainsborough Studios in north London in 1938.

By the late 1930s the British film industry had experienced many ups and downs and Hitchcock had begun to receive lucrative offers from the United States. The offers finally became too tempting to resist and, in March 1939, Hitchcock left Britain aboard the *Queen Mary* for America. Here his talent flourished and he became a top director, working for a range of film studios, which included the prestigious Universal, Paramount and Warner.

"Hitch", as he liked to be known, died in 1980, only three months after receiving his knighthood and in a way this marked the end of a chapter in east London's film history but, like many books, a sequel could emerge. A new east London film studio has been established on Three Mills Island at Bromley-by-Bow in the London borough of Newham and is successfully producing material for cinema and television.

REFERENCES

O'Brien, Margaret & Holland, Julia, "Picture Shows, the Early Film Industry in Walthamstow", *History Today*, February 1987.

Sadler, Nigel & Coxon, Victoria, *Alfred Hitchcock, From Leytonstone to Hollywood,* Vestry House Museum, London, 1999.

Tonkin, W.G.S., *Showtime in Walthamstow*, Occasional Paper No.9, Walthamstow Antiquarian Society, Walthamstow, 1967.

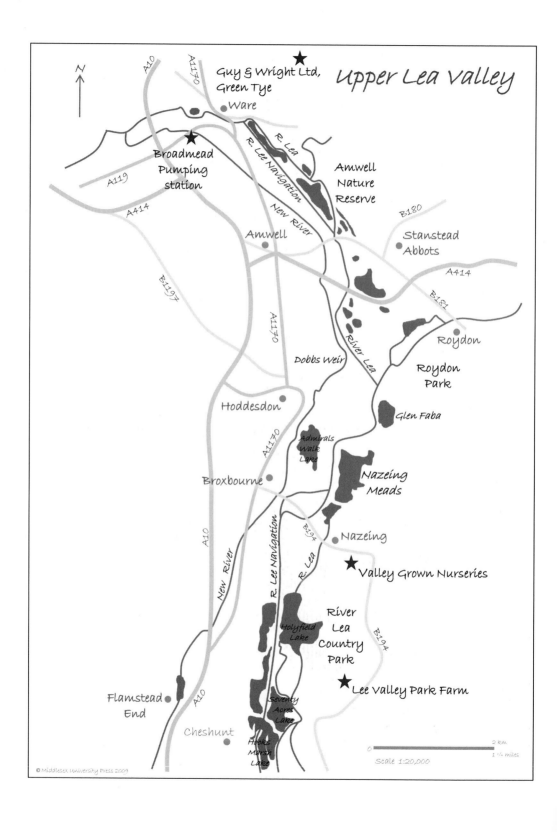

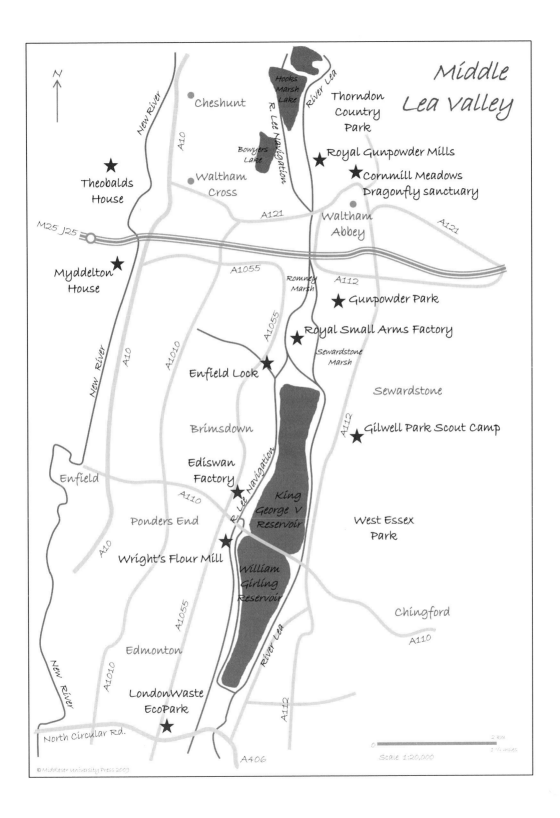

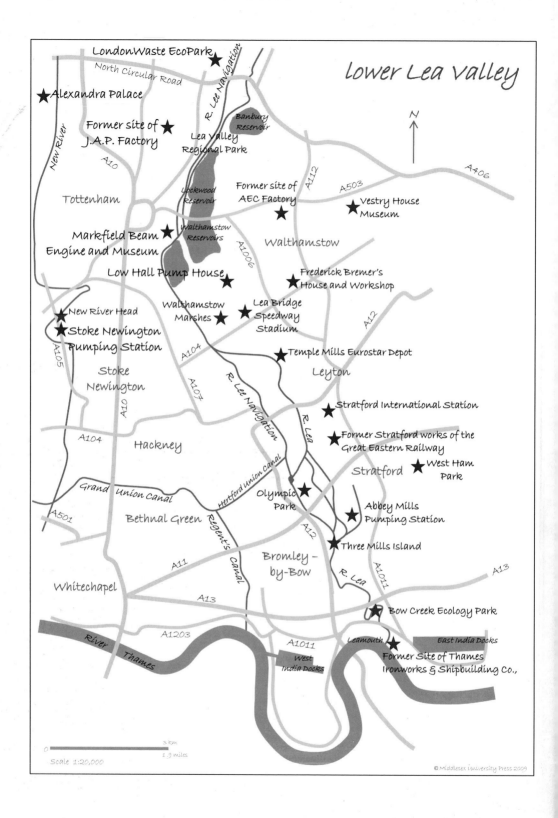

Lower Lea Valley

LondonWaste EcoPark ★

North Circular Road

R. Lee Navigation

★ Alexandra Palace

Former site of ★
J.A.P. Factory

Banbury
Reservoir

Lea Valley
Regional Park

N

A406

New River

A10

Tottenham

Lockwood
Reservoir

Former site of
AEC Factory
★

A112

A503

★ Vestry House
Museum

Markfield Beam ★
Engine and Museum

Walthamstow
Reservoirs

Walthamstow

A1006

Low Hall Pump House
★

Frederick Bremer's
★ House and Workshop

New River Head
★ ★
Stoke Newington
Pumping Station

A105

Stoke
Newington

A10

Walthamstow
Marshes ★

★ Lea Bridge
Speedway
Stadium

A104

A107

R. Lee Navigation

A12

★ Temple Mills Eurostar Depot

Leyton

Hackney

A104

★ Stratford International Station

R. Lea

★ Former Stratford works of the
Great Eastern Railway

Stratford

★ West Ham
Park

Grand Union Canal

A501

Hertford Union Canal

Regent's Canal

Bethnal Green

Olympic ★
Park

A12

★ Abbey Mills
Pumping Station

A11

Bromley –
by-Bow

★ Three Mills Island

Whitechapel

A13

R. Lea

A1011

A13

★ Bow Creek Ecology Park

A1203

River Thames

A1011

Leamouth

East India Docks

★ Former Site of Thames
Ironworks & Shipbuilding Co.,

West
India Docks

0 _____ 3 km
1.9 miles

Scale 1:20,000